Contents

Preface

I began thinking about this book as an update of *Education, Culture and the National Curriculum* (1989). However, when I started to plan the new book I realised that a change of emphasis would be needed. Not yet another book about the national curriculum, but a new analysis of the relation between school curricula, primary and secondary, and teacher professionalism – even teacher empowerment.

Although the demand for greater parent power in the 1970s and 1980s was inevitable, and in many ways desirable, it was taken down the alluring but inevitably disappointing cul-de-sac of 'choice', when it should have been leading to greater understanding of schools and participation in their work. Parental participation should have been paralleled by a development of teacher professionalism – especially in the area of curriculum assessment and reporting. Unfortunately, what happened from 1979 to 1995 was an unrealistic promotion of parents' interest in choice and 'quality'; and at the very time when teachers were demoralised (after their unsuccessful dispute with government in 1986) an unsatisfactory national curriculum and an even less satisfactory system of assessment was imposed on the profession, ignoring all the lessons learned about the implementation of innovation. Meanwhile, teachers had been increasingly subjected to unfair criticisms from the popular press and politicians ill-informed by extremist political advisors.

Instead of parents and teachers being encouraged to cooperate, they were too often forced into confrontation.

With the Education Reform Act (ERA) 1988 we witnessed a tremendous increase in the centralisation of powers in education, a weakening of local democratic control – the Local Education Authorities – and a concerted attempt to de-professionalise teaching (John Patten's infamous 'mum's army' proposal in 1993 was by no means the most important example).

This book is not an attempt to set the clock back: it presents a view of how teachers might reassert their professional concern for the education process, not least in curriculum and assessment. The book is unashamedly teacher-centred in the sense that it is written from the teacher's point of view, at a time of multiple change which has sometimes bordered on chaos.

There are two central themes running through the book. The first suggests that the most important aspect of being a good professional teacher does not rest on the ability to teach interesting lessons (although that is very important): the most important function of professionalism is having the knowledge and understanding to plan teaching and learning sequentially over a long period of time, and to assess and evaluate the results. A good teacher does not focus on planning a lesson, but on the scheme of work, the syllabus, the curriculum and its assessment.

The second theme is that one of the saddest errors since 1979 has been the undermining of teacher professionalism: a poorly planned national curriculum; an unrealistic and bureaucratic inspection programme following the replacement of HMI by OFSTED; a host of hastily implemented changes which over-burdened teachers; and finally a distortion of the concept of 'partnership' between teachers and the central authority.

The time has come for teachers to work for a better balance: a general teaching council would be a good symbolic achievement, but without real empowerment it would not solve the problem. Lawrence Stenhouse once said *'No curriculum development without teacher development'*; I would like to extend that idea to the principle that there can be no real improvement in the quality of the education system unless we have fully professional teachers who are given shared ownership of the system.

1

Introduction: a top-down national curriculum

For many years before the 1988 Education Act I had argued in favour of some kind of national curriculum or common curriculum (Lawton, 1973). Like many others, I believed that there would be considerable professional advantages in having clearer ideas about what we should be aiming at in our primary and secondary schools for all our pupils. We believed that there would be clear benefits from the development of a carefully planned national policy on the school curriculum and reaching as much agreement as possible, nationally, on aims, purposes, content and assessment.

But when the national curriculum as part of the Education Reform Act (ERA) was revealed in 1988, my colleagues and I were very critical of the proposal (Lawton and Chitty 1988). Why?

It is sometimes argued that in England we have had a long tradition of curricular freedom – that is, unlike many other European countries, we have avoided central control over the curriculum. This is only partly true. In the early nineteenth century the ruling classes generally agreed on a policy of non-interference by government (laissez-faire) which included keeping the state out of education. This goes some way to explaining the fact that we were much slower in developing a national system of education than, for example, France or Prussia. But by the second half of the nineteenth century the view that all education should be *private* (that is, neither funded nor controlled by the state) had given way to what I have described elsewhere as a *minimalist* position (Lawton, 1994). This second stage accepted that a modern industrial society could not avoid having an national education system, but minimalists advocated keeping it cheap and basic ('*sound and cheap elementary instruction to all classes of the people'*, Newcastle Report, 1862). Part of the minimalists' system of control was a very basic elementary curriculum linked to payment by results – a policy always opposed by teachers and their professional associations. Similarly, after the 1902 Act, which established maintained secondary schools, the curriculum was tightly controlled by the Secondary Regulations 1904.

Post-war planning

By the time of World War Two (1939–45) the minimalist view was giving way to more democratic ideas about education. Wartime egalitarian attitudes encouraged criticism of a system which segregated children educationally according to the class or wealth of their parents, with only a slender ladder of opportunity from elementary to secondary education allowing some 'poor' children the possibility of changing their class. The 1944 Education Act provided free secondary education for all. This was a major step forward, but lacked clear aims for secondary education – and there was no curriculum policy. For some this was regarded as the golden age of teacher control of the curriculum, but there was, as we shall see, a price to pay for this lack of central policy. Minimalism gave way to a third stage – *pluralism* (different kinds of school and curricula for different types of children). There was still no clear idea of curriculum entitlement, and some children in both primary and secondary schools were certainly given curricula which were inferior. Diversity did not always produce excellence.

By the 1960s and 1970s two trends could be observed. First, more and more Local Education Authorities (LEAs) were moving towards secondary comprehensive schools, irrespective of the political party in control. I refer to this stage as *comprehensive planning* (a single model of schooling for all children). The second trend was for the central authority in education to perceive the need for some kind of national guidance on the curriculum. A small Curriculum Study Group was established by a Conservative government in 1962, which gave way to the more representative Schools Council for Curriculum and Examinations in 1964. Shortly afterwards, Her Majesty's Inspectorate (HMI) began developing ideas about the curriculum, and the HMI publication group were eventually responsible for several influential pamphlets.

Political ideologies

After 1979 the trends towards comprehensive planning and a central view on curriculum were complicated by party politics. Many educationists who had mapped the progression from a *private* system, to *minimalism*, and then *pluralism* and finally to *comprehensive planning* – irrespective of the party in government – were speculating about what might come next. During the 1960s and 1970s, the main debate was between pluralists and comprehensive planners. But after 1979 there was a regression to older – some had thought obsolete – forms of educational thinking. A lesson to be learned from that period (1979 onwards) is that when ideologies such as privatising and minimalism seem to have disappeared, they have not necessarily gone for ever – they have simply sunk into the deep structure of political and educational thinking (Lawton, 1994). Certainly, after the 1979 Election, Conservatives with extreme right-wing views on education felt fewer inhibitions about raising their voices. There were struggles between privatisers and minimalists within the Conservative Party, and between privatisers and pluralists; but there were no Tory comprehensive planners.

By the 1980s the arguments for a national curriculum included a mixture of ideological positions, not all of them represented in the Conservative Party:

1   All children should have a right of access to a worthwhile curriculum (the Entitlement view of some HMI).
2   There ought to be as much consensus as possible nationally on the aims and objectives of compulsory education.
3   An egalitarian view stressing the desirability of equality of access to educational chances, reducing local differences in quality.
4   Common schools should transmit a common culture by means of a common curriculum.
5   That it is important for all schools to share common standards ensuring reasonable levels of teacher expectations.
6   That a national curriculum facilitates the geographic mobility of pupils' parents.
7   A national curriculum increases the accountability of schools and teachers.
8   A national curriculum would increase economic efficiency and competitiveness.

The fact that Kenneth Baker, Secretary of State for Education (1986–1989), seemed more interested in the last four of the above arguments might have been seen as a warning of the kind of curriculum that was to be imposed after an extremely short consultation period in 1987. Some suggested that the national curriculum as it emerged in 1987 and 1988 was a political and bureaucratic curriculum. But why did teachers not resist this unsatisfactory proposal and insist on a national curriculum which was professionally planned?

There are several reasons for the fact that teachers were pushed into the sidelines in 1988. First, teachers had been weakened by an unsuccessful dispute about pay and conditions ending in 1986; they were demoralised and disorganised. Second, teachers were not united: it was not until 1993 that all six teachers' professional organisations briefly acted in concert and boycotted national curriculum assessment. Third, teachers in general may have lacked sufficient theoretical understanding of all the issues surrounding a national curriculum which was intended to be assessed at ages 7, 11, 14 and 16. Some intuitively opposed the idea of testing at 7; others feared that an assessed national curriculum might be over-detailed, over-prescriptive and geared to produce misleading league tables. But there was no view of curriculum theory which united the teaching profession and enabled them to oppose a national curriculum which eventually cost more than £500m before it came so close to disaster that it had to be submitted to the famous Dearing Review.

In some respects, the lack of teacher consensus on curriculum was not surprising, because so-called experts had themselves often been divided or unclear about crucial issues. The following discussion of the 'curriculum and assessment problem' is included partly to explain why the Baker 1988 curriculum failed, but also to clarify the post-Dearing role of teachers in curriculum planning.

Part of the Dearing (1994) message was that the national curriculum should not be seen as the *whole* curriculum, and that it would be the responsibility of teachers in their schools to plan a coherent whole curriculum, filling in the gaps between the ten 'foundation' subjects (see below) in such a way as to produce a unique plan for a particular school situation. The buck had been passed; but perhaps this was a real chance for teacher empowerment.

There are four approaches to curriculum design, which may be described in the following way:

1   The **content** approach.
2   The **process** approach.
3   Curriculum **objectives**.
4   The **assessment**-based curriculum.

It is clear that those who advised Kenneth Baker were not well informed about the issues and problems associated with each of those four models.

1   The content approach

This can be exemplified by the traditional examination syllabus (e.g. GCE A level), which consists of a simple list of topics to be covered, without any attempt to explain or justify the content selected. The emphasis is often (but not necessarily) on memorisation of facts, and the regurgitation of that information in written examination papers. Disadvantages of this approach include the lack of teacher control over both curriculum and assessment, and the fact that the examination dominating the curriculum often involves luck – not *all* of the topics can be included on any examination paper, so the sampling of content involves chance rather than comprehensive coverage. From a planning point of view, the main problem is the lack of justification of the content chosen: it is taken for granted or simply accepted as part of a tradition which has stood the test of time. For that reason the approach is often part of a traditional, 'classical humanist', ideology of education.

Any curriculum must contain content of some kind – but should professional teachers accept a curriculum simply in terms of content to be covered? And surely we should at least ask *'Why this content rather than that?'* as part of a rational planning exercise. The content approach is much in evidence in the 1988 national curriculum, and it would seem that the ten subjects were unquestioningly accepted as traditional content.

2   The process approach

This model is favoured by 'progressive' teachers in both primary and secondary schools. They maintain that memorising facts or other kinds of information is less important than developing understanding of various kinds. This model involves selecting certain kinds of knowledge and experience either because they are interesting or worthwhile in their own right or because they open up new experiences, new kinds of knowledge, new methods of learning. Pedagogy or teaching *method* is a very important aspect of this kind of curriculum. In its extreme form, the teacher might even avoid a fixed curriculum altogether, preferring to concentrate on topics chosen by pupils. But that would be an extreme form of the process approach – not one that I would recommend.

Less extreme versions of this approach would emphasise structured learning. For example, Bruner, in a famous book *The Process of Education* (1960), stressed the importance of the structure of the discipline in terms of key concepts, ideas and processes which should be tackled at the right time and in the correct sequence:

❻ *The importance of structure*
The first object of any act of learning, over and beyond the pleasure it may give, is that it should serve us in the future. Learning should not only take us somewhere; it should allow us later to go further more easily. There are two ways in which learning serves the future. One is through its specific applicability to tasks that are highly similar to those we originally learned to perform. Psychologists refer to this phenomenon as specific transfer of training; perhaps it should be called the extension of habits or associations. Its utility appears to be limited in the main to what we usually speak of as skills. Having learned how to hammer nails, we are better able later to learn how to hammer tacks or chip wood. Learning in school undoubtedly creates skills of a kind that transfers to activities encountered later, either in school or after. A second way in which earlier learning renders later performance more efficient is through what is conveniently called non-specific transfer or, more accurately, the transfer of principles and attitudes.

The motivation of the pupil and the method of learning are important, but they must be closely related to the structure of the content. Such a curriculum would be based on theories of child development and learning at various ages, integrated with the careful planning of subject-matter presentation. The emphasis is on sequence and structure (and, in Bruner's case, the notion of the spiral curriculum: the same concepts crop up on several occasions, but with increasing degrees of complexity to match the conceptual development of the learners). This curriculum fits in well with the overall idea of curriculum planning and design – concepts and ideas are seen as building blocks which have to be laid in a carefully planned sequence. Even that metaphor is misleading, because those who advocate the process model would emphasise the interactive and dynamic nature of teaching and learning – much more complex than laying bricks in a preconceived order.

One difficulty of this approach, apart from its complexity, is that sophisticated models like Bruner's are often condemned along with simplistic child-centred approaches where the curriculum may be almost non-existent.

Although the main emphasis of the national curriculum was on content, there is some evidence – but not enough – of process thinking in some of the national curriculum attainment targets, as well as in the TGAT assessment model which will be discussed later.

3   The objectives approach

The main problem with this approach lies in the ambiguity of the word *'objectives'*. For some behaviourists, objectives must always be 'behavioural objectives' – that is, prespecified in terms of measurable changes in behaviour. The emphasis is on changes in student behaviour rather than on the intentions of the teacher. This view of curriculum planning was attacked years ago by Stenhouse (1975) and others because it fragmented the learning process and devalued the complexity of human behaviour; for similar reasons, the behaviourist view of learning was dismissed by philosophers and psychologists alike (e.g. Sockett, 1980, Chomsky, 1959). The strict view of planning by behavioural objectives is probably quite dead, although behavioural techniques might be useful for some limited purposes at low levels of skill learning and behaviour modification.

Further along the continuum we find objectives which are precise but not behavioural. This planning model has been found useful for certain kinds of specific training, but is usually considered too rigid for more open learning situations. If you want to teach someone to type, it may make sense to have very specific and measurable targets (objectives): 50 words per minute with no errors after 100 hours of training. But if we try to apply that kind of formula to appreciating poetry or understanding historical events, the model breaks down: the situation is much more complex and we have to plan learning quite differently. We may still choose to use the word *objective*, but if so, it takes on a different meaning. Skilbeck (1984), for example, has argued that objectives can be a useful part of the planning process, provided we are careful and clear about what we mean. The key question is always how precise or specific the objectives should be. This is another problem to which we will have to return.

Another difficulty with objectives as the basis of curriculum design is that we need to be able to relate them carefully to more general aims and values. In other words, we cannot begin with objectives: we must derive our objectives from something else at a higher level of planning. This was one of the errors of the 1988 national curriculum.

4   The assessment-based approach

Finally, there are some who would advocate planning a curriculum starting from (and finishing with) assessment. It is doubtful whether this is a model in its own right, rather than a variant of the objectives model in which objectives are expressed in terms of learning targets which are to be assessed in a clear and specific way. From a planning point of view, however, there are some important features of the assessment-based approach.

This model might seem to have certain advantages of presenting clear tasks for teachers and learners, except that if the stress on assessment outweighs the underlying curricular purposes, there are dangers. There is a temptation to assess what is easy or most convenient to *test*, rather than what is most important to *learn*. If the assessment is of the kind now referred to as 'high stakes assessment', there are other problems of distortion – students may be tempted to cheat, and teachers may be distracted from their real purpose in order to 'teach to the test' and produce 'good results' (see Chapter 7).

At this stage I would like to emphasise one very important point: with the doubtful exception of the content approach, all the other models beg the fundamental question of *'Why?'*. There is a missing first stage in every model: the *justification* of content, process or objectives in terms of aims based on values or principles. I say that the content approach may be an exception, because some traditionalists would argue that we have no need to ask 'why?' because the school curriculum has evolved over centuries and should be allowed to continue undisturbed. I suggest that such a view does not stand up to rational enquiry: many writers have commented on the phenomenon of 'curriculum lag and inertia' or the tendency for curriculum to be much too slow to catch up with other social and technological changes. Furthermore, if we are discussing the national curriculum 1988, it would be impossible to advance the 'hallowed tradition' argument because the national curriculum was itself an attempt to change the status quo.

The national curriculum

One problem in 1988 was that it was never clear whether the planning was based on *content* (subjects) or *objectives* (attainment targets), and, in addition, it was never made clear where either came from: the underlying values and aims were not specified. A further difficulty (to be explored later) was that the concept of attainment targets (ATs) was just as ambiguous as the term 'objective'. ATs were treated differently by the various Subject Working Groups, and at crucial times they changed in meaning or specificity. Teachers were handed down a curriculum that was planned in great haste, with no clear aims and values, and without a coherent design, and were expected to teach and assess it after minimal opportunities to prepare for it. A recipe for disaster!

The 1988 national curriculum was an uneasy mixture of all four models, with insufficient attention being paid to the problem of compatibility. It was presented as four separate but inter-related elements:

1 The **foundation subjects** (a strong emphasis on traditional content:
   the three 'core subjects' English, mathematics and science, plus
   technology, history, geography, art, music and physical education);
2 **Attainment targets** for each subject (objectives – but how specific
   were they to be?);
3 **Programmes of Study** for each subject (mostly content with a little
   process);
4 **Assessment** at 7, 11, 14 and 16 (which some suspected would
   become the dominant element; it did, but it was also much distorted
   in the early 1990s).

The **content** basis was thus very strong, but the ten subjects were not
justified in any way, nor related to any more general aims or values; there
was no apology for missing parts and no links between subjects. It was left
to the National Curriculum Council (NCC) to try later to weld the
curriculum together by means of *cross-curricular themes* (see later chapters).

The **process** approach was least in evidence, but not entirely absent in
some foundation subjects in the national curriculum. Process was always
seen by traditional Conservatives as trendy and suspect (part of a left-
wing educationists' conspiracy – see Lawton, 1994).

The **objectives** model was strongly represented in 1988, but it was
never clear how close the objectives were intended to be to behavioural
objectives. There was much talk about the curriculum and assessment
being criterion-referenced, but from the beginning some objectives – in
the form of Statements of Attainment for each Level of Attainment
Targets – were very vague, and later moved even further in the direction
of being general rather than specific. This is, of course, not an academic
quibble: the level of specificity of an objective makes considerable
difference to the curriculum design, as well as to how the curriculum
should be assessed.

The **assessment** scheme for the national curriculum was originally
entrusted to Professor Paul Black and his Task Group for Assessment
and Testing (TGAT). This Group had a very difficult task to complete in
a very short time – about six months. They produced a model which
avoided many of the features feared by educationists, such as pass/fail
and repeating a year's work (the French *redoublement* pattern). TGAT
produced a model which emphasised both progression and
differentiation, as well as attempting to provide the kind of assessment
which would enable teachers to use assessment diagnostically whilst
producing the kind of statistical data required by bureaucrats and the
league tables demanded by politicians.

A key feature of the model was the central role of teachers in the assessment process. TGAT intended that teacher assessment would be central, but would be moderated in order to achieve national standards. Unfortunately, the government never accepted the notion of teacher moderation and gave far greater weight to external tests – the Standard Assessment Tasks (SATs). This was eventually to become such a complex bureaucratic system that it collapsed under its own weight.

The result in the years following 1988 was an incoherent compromise – a national curriculum which did not stand up to theoretical scrutiny, and, more importantly, failed in practice.

Most teachers and other professionals took the view that once the national curriculum was made law (after 1988) their duty was to try to make the curriculum work despite all its imperfections. It was not easy. Difficulties began almost immediately.

Part of the grand scheme was that the Secretary of State appointed a Working Group for each Foundation Subject to draw up Programmes of Study and Attainment Targets. This led to at least two problems. First, each group of subject experts tended to be enthusiasts who inevitably prescribed more content for their own subject than any timetable could sustain. Second, there was no time for one subject group to consult, let alone cooperate with, any other group. Hence there were differences in the interpretation of Programmes of Study and Attainment Targets, and even inconsistencies between what was prescribed at one level for one subject and another level for another subject (e.g. pupils were required to use mathematics for their science which was not planned in the mathematics programme until a year or two later).

And the assumption was made that the ten-level model of assessment was equally suitable for all subjects. But English and history were never happy with the model (see Cox, 1995). When it came to assessment, the fears voiced by my late colleague, Desmond Nuttall (1989) were justified: namely, that assessment would be distorted by the league tables.

The TGAT model was potentially very useful: it avoided the problem of end of year failure and gave due emphasis to progression and differentiation. But Mrs Thatcher tells us in her autobiography (1993) that she was always opposed to the TGAT model. Kenneth Baker stood his ground, and at first had his own way, but in the end the contradictions were too great. For some Conservatives the national curriculum was mainly a means of providing parents with market information. If parents were to choose, they must have data about good schools and bad schools – league tables. This distorted the assessment process (the TGAT model) in a number of ways: first, there was pressure on the teachers to show that their class was doing well (the problem of high-stakes assessment, mentioned earlier). Second, there was pressure on the School Examinations and Assessment Council (SEAC) to convert the TGAT methodology into a very precise testing machine providing results which were at once highly accurate and capable of aggregation, thus providing information immediately meaningful to parents in their search for the best school.

This desire for 100 per cent accuracy and 'transparency' was always doomed to failure. Assessment of students of any age is not an exact science (as studies of GCSE and A level have shown); with Key Stage 1 (7 year olds) assessment there were particular difficulties. The first TGAT report had included an excellent section on the problems of reaching uniformity of standards. The report concluded that the only workable method would be for teachers to assess their own pupils and for the standardisation of levels to be achieved by group moderation procedures. This is an expensive method (but not as expensive as the alternative turned out to be). Group moderation has the advantage of giving some ownership of the assessment process to teachers themselves; in GCSE it has also been shown to be the most effective method of INSET or professional development for teachers. But this professional solution was never accepted by the Conservative Government, and that part of the TGAT model was rejected. Instead, external markers were paid to check the marking standards of teachers for the Standard Assessment Tasks (SATs).

Another early mistake was made in the planning of Key Stage 1 assessment. Each subject was broken down into Attainment Targets (ATs) – for example, in English there were ATs for Reading, Writing and Speaking & listening). Each AT was sub-divided into ten levels, with several Statements of Attainment (SoAs) to indicate achievement at each level. So far so good, but in the search for scientific accuracy, teachers were required to make individual judgements for every SoA for every AT level covered. The alternative, later taken up by Dearing (1994), was for teachers to make a single global judgment for each Attainment Target indicating the level reached by each pupil. In 1994 SoAs were abolished and replaced by Level Descriptions. Since for the average child the difference between level 2 and level 3 represented the equivalent of two years' development, making a *global* judgment would not have been difficult. But in 1991 primary teachers were required instead to provide detailed information for *every* child's performance in English, maths, science and technology for *every* SoA for *every* AT level. This was a bureaucratic task of nightmare proportions, with the promise of teachers having to carry out the same procedures for other subjects in later years.

That problem alone would have been enough to cause chaos, but the Secretary of State, Kenneth Clarke, disregarded the advice of his group of professionals on SEAC and decided that the meaningful but time-consuming SATs would be replaced by more conventional paper-and-pencil tests. He dismissed the professionally designed SATs as *'elaborate nonsense'*.

The Dearing Review

The new testing at Key Stage 1 remained time-consuming, but was now much less valid: teachers were no longer convinced that the tests were assessing what they were intended to test. At Key Stage 3, teachers of fourteen-year-old pupils were perhaps even more dissatisfied with the new 'simpler' tests that had replaced SATs. Secondary school teachers of English, in particular, were insulted by the 1993 tests. Soon primary as well as secondary teachers, supported by their Headteachers' organisations, boycotted all tests at Key Stages 1 and 3. All six teacher unions were united in their opposition. Efforts were made to declare the boycott illegal, but the teachers' action continued and was often supported by the parents. Sir Ron Dearing was called in as a trouble-shooter, and before his Review was complete, the Secretary of State then responsible, John Patten, had been returned to the backbenches.

How the immediate disaster was averted by Dearing will be discussed later. At this stage, it is enough to note that he reduced the national curriculum content quite substantially for primary and secondary schools, and instead emphasised the responsibility of schools themselves for converting the national curriculum into a coherent whole curriculum. Schools after 1994 would somehow have to make sense of the national curriculum, and use it as the basis for their own school-based curriculum design.

OFSTED

Meanwhile, the Education (Schools) Act 1992 had privatised the inspection process. The number of HMI was greatly reduced and the Office for Standards in Education (OFSTED) became the 'independent' body responsible for contracting independent teams to inspect primary and secondary schools. HMI/OFSTED trained the new inspectors and required them to work to a new *Framework for the Inspection of Schools*. The requirements of the Framework covered much more than the national curriculum:

❝ The function of an inspection under Section 9 ... is to report on:

- ■ the quality of the education provided by the school;
- ■ the educational standards achieved in the school;
- ■ whether the financial resources ... are managed efficiently; and
- ■ the spiritual, moral, social and cultural (SMSC) development of pupils at the school.

That last requirement provides another reason for schools to begin to think carefully about the problem of school-based planning. What sort of curriculum design and implementation would satisfy the new breed of inspectors? More importantly, how should teachers in primary and secondary schools go about designing a curriculum appropriate for pupils facing the twenty-first century?

Summary

These questions will be addressed in the chapters which follow. But we are left with the fundamental problem that the national curriculum (1988) was a top-down, political-bureaucratic programme imposed on teachers who were marginalised by the whole 1988 Act, which was deliberately anti-professional in several ways. It appealed to market forces rather than planning, and to parental choice rather than the professionalism of teachers whose status was reduced to that of employees required to carry out orders.

The real value of the Dearing Review – as we shall see – was that teachers were not only consulted but listened to, and more space was provided for teachers to develop school curricula professionally. The revised national curriculum was far from perfect, but it provided a useful springboard for the process of designing professional school-based curricula in every school.

2

Planning a curriculum: teacher professionalism or teacher-proof materials?

Chapter 1 included a reference to Sir Ron Dearing's redefinition of the national curriculum in such a way as to give schools additional planning responsibilities. We should not exaggerate this change: the Kenneth Baker national curriculum had implicitly argued that the national curriculum was not the whole curriculum, and that some scope would be left for school planning; but as the national curriculum emerged after 1988, it increasingly became more like a total programme (using all the time available, even if it did not provide a coherent, broad and balanced curriculum). The Dearing Review made a difference in two ways: it reduced the time allocated to the national curriculum; and when questioned by interest groups about serious gaps in the national curriculum, the official response by the School Curriculum and Assessment Authority (SCAA) was that such matters as citizenship, moral education or health were for the school to incorporate into their own school-based whole curriculum plan. The national curriculum was seen as the statutory minimum; the school would be concerned with planning a much richer total experience.

Further weight was given to the notion of the school-based whole curriculum by changes in arrangements for inspecting schools. The 1992 Education (Schools) Act replaced the process of HMI school inspection by a privatised system of independent inspectors trained by the Office of the Chief Inspector (later called the Office for Standards in Education – OFSTED). The Chief Inspector and the remaining HMI produced instructions for the new style inspections in the form of a

Framework and a *Handbook.* One important feature of the new inspection regime was that schools would be judged not only on pupil achievements in national curriculum subjects, but on the overall spiritual, moral, social and cultural (SMSC) development of the pupils. Unfortunately, there are no clear guidelines about what constitutes such development, and the *Framework* (1994) provided only negative indicators:

> Pupils' spiritual, moral, social and cultural development: very poor provision for these aspects of pupils' development; poor assemblies; abrasive and confrontational relationships with pupils; regular disruptive behaviour; high levels of truancy; poor attendance by a substantial proportion of pupils or a particular group of pupils; high levels of exclusion; pupils at physical or emotional risk from other pupils or adults in the school; high level of racial tension or harassment ...

Presumably the manifestation of positive signs of this desirable development would involve certain values expressed in what has increasingly been referred to as *school culture* or *ethos.* A good curriculum design would attempt to make such values explicit and also relate them to the aims and objectives of a curriculum plan.

Schools were thus left with a major task of curriculum design. Pessimists will say that teachers have been passed a poisoned chalice; optimists talk in terms of teacher empowerment. In any case, we are back to the question *'How to plan a curriculum?'.*

Curriculum planning

In Chapter 1 I described very briefly four models or approaches and suggested that the fourth approach (assessment-based) was often regarded as a version of the objectives model. I also suggested that none of the four approaches could be regarded as complete, because a vital first stage was missing. Where did the content, process or objectives come from? How could they be justified? Why chemistry but not astronomy? Was Richard Rogers (1995) right to ask for architecture to be included in the school curriculum? If so, why? Why is religious education compulsory in England but forbidden in many other countries? What are the principles and values behind such decisions (or non-decisions)?

One of the problems of modern industrial society is that work tends to take on a very powerful significance for adults. Employers and parents often see schooling largely in terms of preparation for work. This is an incomplete view of education, since work is only one of many features of the adult world. A related danger is that the distinction between education and training becomes confused.

In recent years there has been a good deal of discussion about *education* and *training*, sometimes contrasting the two words, sometimes advocating the complete abolition of the distinction. It has also been suggested that schools are failing because they have not provided the trained manpower needed by industry and commerce.

In any discussion of curriculum planning it is important to preserve the distinction between the two concepts, but to emphasise that some worthwhile activities in schools may be a mixture of both. It is also important to avoid the assumption that education is good and training is inferior.

Training is the appropriate word when we are concerned with a specific skill or set of skills with clear criteria for right and wrong outcomes. The army has weapons training instructors not weapons education teachers. They have clear criteria about how to hold a rifle, how to aim, how to squeeze (not pull) the trigger, how to strip and clean a rifle. There is no room for any debate about methods – there is a right way and a wrong way. Successful performance can be measured without difficulty. Training is a closed system; progress takes place within a deficit model – errors are easily identified and put right. A 100 per cent success rate is the required goal.

Education, on the other hand, is open-ended. Not all objectives can be defined or prespecified with complete precision, although we may want as much precision as possible. There are criteria to indicate good and bad procedures, but there will not necessarily be a single correct answer, nor one right way of performing. Good performance and improved achievement can be recognised, perhaps even measured, but with less precision and certainty. Indeed, one of the goals of education should be the encouragement of tolerance of uncertainty and ambiguity in appropriate circumstances. If a student stated that the French Revolution started in 1815, he is certainly wrong, although there is a good deal of doubt about when it did start; and if we move on to a discussion of the causes of the French Revolution, there is even more uncertainty. There is not just one right answer, partly because important events in history can rarely be related to one single 'cause' or event. Similarly, in English literature, who can say that Olivier's interpretation of Hamlet was more 'correct' than Gielgud's? And words like *interpretation, taste,* and *style* are much more difficult to cope with in assessment terms than rifle shots hitting a target. That is one of the problems of public examinations and one reason for debates about the results and standards in GCSE and A level almost every year.

But the idea that training is an *inferior* activity should be avoided. Training is an essential aspect of educational planning and is an important part of many school activities. It is a question of appropriateness rather than superiority/inferiority. It is true that a dog can be trained but not educated; it is also true that most travellers would prefer to travel in an aeroplane with a well-trained pilot rather than a well-educated one. Some kinds of training are complex and demanding. It has become fashionable to talk of teacher education rather than teacher training, but for some aspect of teacher preparation the word *training* might be more appropriate. However, teachers need to be well educated as well as well trained. Most of those involved in higher education would like to believe that the airline pilot would be a better human being if he were educated as well as trained. But the priority is clear. Training is, however, morally neutral, whereas education implies improvement: it is possible to train an individual to be an efficient torturer, but you could not make him better educated in that way.

There is, however, another problem with the education/training distinction. The difference which is clear in English but not in some other languages has reinforced a social tendency to regard *vocational education* as an inferior version of *liberal education*. Vocational education has tended to be seen as a sub-standard route for those who cannot cope with academic education. This is a distortion: the hidden distinction is not between academic and vocational but between high status occupations and those of lower status. We make a similar linguistic distinction between *professions* and *jobs* which is hard to justify on grounds other than status. The fact that we have professional training for doctors and lawyers which is associated with universities whereas electricians and plumbers are trained elsewhere is of social and historical rather than educational significance. The result has been the development of a tradition which unfortunately associates education with the academic and abstract rather than with practical kinds of knowledge.

We shall return to that topic later in the context of discussions about vocational options for the 14–16 age group. The problem with such options is not that they are oriented towards work, but is that in the past they have been taught in a way which did not encourage educational processes of thought and reflection. To see vocational courses as in themselves necessarily inferior to academic courses is quite wrong, just as it would be wrong to assume that a medical degree was inferior to a degree in history or English literature. A 'professional' degree can be just as educational if it is carefully planned and well taught.

It is also important to stress that for some educational processes training is a prerequisite. For example, elementary reading and arithmetic involve training in basic skills; so does learning a modern language or playing the piano. One legitimate criticism of some schools is that they have not paid enough attention to skills and training: they take them for granted when they should be more aware of them as desirable objectives. But it is equally mistaken to think of all education simply as acquiring skills.

USA experience

Similarly, there is a view of education and curriculum planning (in my view completely misguided) which claims that all learning processes can be reduced to a series of behavioural objectives, which can be mastered as a result of training and then measured in terms of performance outcomes. If this were true, education as well as training could be reduced to a very simple mechanistic formula. That approach can be traced back to Franklin Bobbitt (1918), who was a superintendent of schools in the USA. He wanted to develop a scientifically planned curriculum by means of what he called 'activity analysis':

> Developed by Franklin Bobbitt and W. W. Charters, the method activity analysis came to be cloaked as the scientific way to build a curriculum. According to Bobbitt, life consists of the performance of specific activities; if education is preparation for life, then it must prepare for these specific activities; these activities, however numerous, are definite and particularised, and can be taught; therefore, these activities will be the objectives of the curriculum. (Tanner and Tanner, 1980)

Curriculum building was, for Bobbitt, the job of an 'educational engineer' (Bobbitt, 1924). He was attempting to apply to education the techniques of the industrial psychologist F.W. ('Speedy') Taylor. The approach rested on an assumption that each area of 'life activity' consisted of a list of specifiable components.

Even if that had been true and it had been possible to translate those components into a curriculum, such educational engineering would have resulted in a static system; there was no allowance for social change. Bobbitt also intended that educational goals and standards should be set, not by educationists, but by businessmen. When Bobbitt applied activity analysis and job analysis to curriculum construction, he estimated that what schools needed to teach could be reduced to about 30,000 specific mechanical skills. At that time behaviourist psychology was fashionable, and it provided a convenient but inadequate theory to support the

Bobbitt curriculum. The formula was never seriously implemented on a wide scale, but has been revived from time to time, sometimes as a means of criticising educational practices. There are some similarities between the Bobbitt ideas and some of the Conservative reforms since 1979, and they were not totally absent from the thinking behind the national curriculum in 1988.

Tyler

In was not until the late 1940s that a less extreme version of the objectives approach was seriously discussed. Tyler (1949) suggested four fundamental questions for curriculum planning:

- What educational purposes should a school seek to attain?
- What educational experiences can be provided that are likely to attain those purposes?
- How can those educational experiences be effectively organised?
- How can we determine whether those purposes are being attained?

Tyler's book was very influential; but it is important to distinguish between Tyler's ideas and the more extreme versions put forward by such writers as Mager (1962) and Popham (1969).

Mager (1962), in a book on programmed learning, demanded that objectives be specified operationally at definite levels of performance; he then extended this demand to cover any educational goals: *'Curriculum objectives must always be prespecified in terms of measurable changes in student behaviour.'*

The change from Tyler's objectives to Mager's behavioural objectives was of considerable significance in the curriculum debate in the 1960s. Popham (1969) sometimes appeared to disagree with the extreme position of Mager, but he also wanted to limit the meaning of objectives to behavioural objectives. That narrow definition was similar to Bobbitt's desire to separate means and ends – that is, instruction and curriculum.

Other curriculum theorists such as Hilda Taba (1962) used *objectives* in a wider sense, but by the early 1970s there was a movement among US curriculum writers demanding that the only meaningful interpretation of objectives was *behavioural* objectives. Curriculum conferences witnessed a number of enthusiasts with lapel badges and car stickers saying *'Help stamp out non-behavioural objectives'!*.

Tyler had never adopted such an extreme position, and in 1973 he criticised some versions of his own rationale: in particular he complained about the failure to *'distinguish between the learning of highly specific skills for limited job performance and the more generalised understanding, problem-solving skills and other kinds of behavioural patterns that thoughtful teachers and educators seek to help students develop'* (Tyler, 1973). That distinction is still very relevant today.

Many writers have criticised the behavioural objectives approach to curriculum and to the behaviourist psychology associated with it. One criticism is that many planners tend to take existing objectives for granted, rather than submitting them to critical scrutiny. Curriculum developers often define their task as improving the efficiency of existing programmes, rather than seeking to justify them or to revise them by a consideration of basic principles. Kliebard (1970) said that Tyler's treatment of objectives was no more than a description of the status quo when what was required was a critical analysis of Tyler's three sources of objectives – learners, contemporary life and subject specialists. No attempt was made by Tyler to evaluate their relative importance or to judge specific inputs from any one of the three sources.

❝ To say that educational objectives are drawn from one's philosophy ... is only to say that one must make choices about educational objectives in some way related to one's value structure. This is to say so little about the process of selecting objectives as to be virtually meaningless. One wonders whether the longstanding insistence by curriculum theorists that the first step in making a curriculum be the specification of objectives has any merit whatsoever. (Kliebard, 1970)

Stenhouse (1970) also opposed the view that an objective should be stated in terms of a student's behavioural change rather than in terms of an activity to be carried out by a teacher. He rejected the assumption that teachers should always know exactly what response would be appropriate for every student; he also rejected the related assumptions about the nature of knowledge.

Equally strong objections have been levelled against behaviourist psychology as a basis of the behavioural objectives approach to curriculum. Skinner (1968) has been criticised for reducing pupils to mechanical objects and devaluing the work of teachers. Skinner described the teacher as one who *'arranges the contingencies of reinforcement'* by which pupils are automatically conditioned for prespecified behavioural changes. This mechanistic and atomistic view of human life is dangerously utopian, treating the education of human beings as if it were the same as training Skinner's pigeons to play ping pong.

The major error of those curriculum theorists basing their planning on behavioural objectives was that they tried to make the model apply to the whole of the curriculum rather than to small parts of it. Because the behavioural objectives model worked well for teaching simple skills, some theorists made the simplistic assumption that it would work equally well for the whole educational process. They ignored the difference between education and training and were misled by behavioural psychologists into underestimating the complex nature of human learning. The behavioural objectives model was also related to a narrow industrial concept of education concerned with training for conformity rather than improving the quality of life.

There is a clear need to distinguish objectives from behavioural objectives. Whereas it is unrealistic and even dangerous to attempt to plan a whole curriculum in terms of behavioural objectives, the alternative is not a programme without any goals or purposes. It is important for teachers and students to know where they are going, and the conversion of general aims into objectives is a useful way of clarifying the learning process, setting realistic learning tasks, and relating learning to achievement by an assessment process with helpful feedback.

Skilbeck

Skilbeck (1984) suggested that it is useful for a curriculum to be *planned* in terms of objectives (that is, learning activities or even outcomes) rather than simply to employ very general statements about teacher intentions. Such objectives might be nearer to the closed model of training, or might be more open – for example, concerned with understanding key concepts and ideas.

> We can agree that student performances *(a)* cannot or should not be prespecified in detail and *(b)* are a part but not the whole of what we mean by education. But why should either of these considerations be inconsistent with stating objectives as the directions in which we are trying to guide student learning? **The translation of broad aims into directions and structures for student learning is just what curriculum design is about.** One of the reasons why there is so much justifiable dissatisfaction with schooling is that for large numbers of students this process is still missing out on what is important and valuable for them: by refusing to focus on sound objectives for all may we not be countenancing the continuance of an unfair and inadequate education system?... broadly based, comprehensive objectives in the curriculum need not be confused with detailed inventories of pieces of behaviour. (Skilbeck, 1984, my emphasis)

Curriculum planning is a process of breaking down general aims into a series of short-term experiences, and then rebuilding them into a whole learning experience. We need also to remember that the experience will be different for every student, and it is in this way that the curriculum plan must be linked to the art of the teacher in dealing with individual differences. In that context, the idea of negotiated objectives becomes meaningful within the framework of a common or national curriculum. The learning process must be coherent for every pupil, but it is unlikely that coherence can be achieved in the same way for the whole class.

One problem with the primitive objectives model suggested by Bobbitt and others was that it was a completely static model; another was that it was an extreme version of a top-down curriculum. Teachers would have no ownership whatsoever of the curriculum: they would be routine workers passing on skills in a completely mechanical way. That view of teachers did not disappear in the 1920s, however: in the 1960s there was much talk of 'teacher-proof materials', and in the 1980s some politicians and others saw the national curriculum as a means of exercising complete control over what teachers taught in the classroom.

This discussion has taken us away from the problem of planning a national curriculum, and back to the problem of school-based implementation of the curriculum plan and the role of the professional teacher.

Summary

This chapter began by accepting the view that the national curriculum should not be regarded as the *whole* curriculum. The reasons for planning in terms of a school-based curriculum were briefly examined – the Dearing Review and OFSTED inspections in particular. A suitable planning model was sought. The behavioural objectives view of curriculum was dismissed as inadequate, despite the strong pressures to move in that direction from government and from those who would like to see the school curriculum more vocationally oriented. It was thought to be inadequate partly because it rests upon the faulty psychological theory of behaviourism and partly because it ignores the all-important first stage of planning – the values and general aims from which content or objectives or processes should be derived.

Skilbeck addressed this problem in a model which began with 'analysing the situation'. The next chapter will describe one method of 'analysing the situation' in the context of a modern, democratic industrial society. This will take us back to the question of school-based planning.

3

Culture and curriculum: teachers, values and cultural analysis

Chapter 2 was concerned with the rejection of the behavioural objectives approach to curriculum planning for two reasons: first, it is based on a narrow and rigid mechanistic view of human learning which is unacceptable to professional teachers; second, it relies on a top-down planning method which deprofessionalises teachers by regarding them as routine workers employed to administer 'teacher-proof' curricula.

An alternative approach to curriculum is to see it as a selection from the culture of society, with teachers (and others) involved in the selection process as well as in its teaching. One of the fascinating aspects of curriculum studies is that for most societies, for many periods in time, schools have operated with curricula which were – in one way or another – inappropriate.

A curriculum fable

✗ Why should this be the case? One reason is the inability of schools to keep up with other changes in society – technological, economic or political. The most famous curriculum fable of all time – 'the sabre-tooth curriculum' – makes the point. This fable concerned a simple, pre-literate society where survival depended on three kinds of skill: spearing fish in the streams, clubbing little woolly horses (for their meat and also for leather for clothing), and frightening away the sabre-tooth tiger with fire.

The school curriculum reflected those survival needs: children were taught to make spears, to keep them sharp and to throw them effectively; they learned how to make clubs and exactly how to use them on the little woolly horses; and finally they were taught how to light fires, and how best to use and transport fire in order to frighten the sabre-tooth tiger.

All was well. Until the climate changed. Then the streams became muddy, so instead of spearing fish the tribesmen had to catch them with nets. The woolly horses moved away; now only antelope roamed the plains, and they were too quick to be caught by clubbing – the tribesmen discovered how to catch them in snares. The sabre-tooth tiger became extinct; now the great danger was the giant brown bear who was not frightened by fire, but could be trapped by digging pits.

The tribal society survived. But the schools carried on teaching the now obsolete skills of fish-spearing, horse-clubbing and fire-lighting. After a while some radical teachers suggested that maybe schools ought to reform the curriculum and teach netting, snaring and pit-digging. But the elders (in the ruling Conservative Party) shook their heads and replied that such a reform would be to disregard the importance of cultural heritage: the new skills were not really educational – they were mere vocational training.

The fable is not entirely fair to those who wish to retain traditional aspects of culture, but it makes the point about the tendency for education to lag behind other kinds of social change. In 1805, for example, Lord Eldon, the Lord Chancellor, ruled that the curriculum of Leeds Grammar School should consist of only Greek and Latin, and it was not until 1840 that the Grammar Schools Act permitted a broader curriculum for such schools. In education, more perhaps than any other institution, there is a tendency for practice to become enshrined as sacred tradition and for everyone involved to resist change. Schools are necessarily conservative institutions, and it is part of their function to preserve important aspects of traditional culture, but they must also have regard for present and future needs.

In a rapidly changing society, there is a need for an institution of some kind to be responsible for keeping the curriculum up to date. But such an institution will also need to develop principles and procedures for analysing social developments and making careful judgments about necessary changes.

The rest of this chapter gives a very brief outline of *cultural analysis* as a means of planning and justifying curriculum change. This also provides a means of transforming a minimal national curriculum (as required by law) into a broader, richer school-based curriculum which is professionally planned by teachers themselves. Such a curriculum will have to be justified to others: parents, governors, OFSTED inspectors and, not least, to the pupils. The reasons for including some aspects of culture and excluding others will need to be made explicit. Making lists of priorities involves value judgments: why, say, is science more important (educationally) than ballroom dancing? Teachers have to be able to *justify* whatever decisions they make.

This chapter begins not with the immediate task of school-based curriculum planning, but by looking more generally at the human situation, at cultural values and the purposes of education. Above all, teachers need to have confidence in the worthwhileness of any curriculum they teach.

In Chapter 2 the distinction was made between narrow behavioural objectives and more broadly based objectives. *Choosing* objectives depends on values: we choose what we think most important. But by what criteria or values? Different societies make different judgments about curriculum, but they all make selections from their culture. One danger is that at times of economic depression there is a tendency to overemphasise the links between education and employment, with the related problem of narrowing the aims of education. This can be avoided by concentrating on more general links between education and culture.

Culture

Culture is one of the most complex concepts in our language, but it is central to the task of curriculum planning. A major difference between animal behaviour and human behaviour is that human beings rely less on instinct than on what they learn from their culture. A bird does not need to learn how to build a nest, but humans have to learn how to use tools, how to employ language, how to know what is appropriate and inappropriate behaviour, and many other aspects of culture. The *disadvantage* is that children are dependent on their parents or other adults for many years; the *advantage* is that human behaviour is more flexible and adaptive – we do not have to do exactly what the previous generation did. Social change is a major feature of human communities but not of animal groups. Both culture and curriculum should be concerned with '*what might be*' as well as '*what is*'.

The word *culture* as used by social scientists embraces everything that has been created by human beings themselves: tools and technology, language and literature, music and art, science and mathematics, attitudes and values – the whole way of life of a society. Any society has the problem of passing on this way of life, or culture, to the next generation. In simple societies, culture is transmitted directly by members of the family or by means of other 'face-to-face' relations. In complex societies, the division of labour and social mobility make it impossible for culture to be passed on entirely by traditional, informal means; the task is partly entrusted to formal education.

Education is concerned with making available to the next generation whatever is regarded as the most valuable aspects of culture. Because schools have limited time and resources, the curriculum needs to be planned to ensure that an appropriate selection from culture is made. Those responsible for making the selection have a duty to demonstrate that it is neither arbitrary nor idiosyncratic. It should be open to rational enquiry and justification, not least because complete agreement about the curriculum – a selection from culture – will rarely be possible.

In order to plan a curriculum based on a justifiable selection from culture, it is necessary to have a process or set of principles by which it can be seen that the selection is being made. That process is referred to as *cultural analysis*. The cultural analysis process which is outlined here cannot claim to be value-free, but can claim to state values explicitly. Justification takes place in a context of values, some of which may be well established societal values enshrined in legislation (such as equal opportunity), others will be more basic human values common to all societies, and some may be values which in a pluralist society may be controversial – but still open to rational enquiry.

Cultural analysis

At the simplest level, cultural analysis for the purpose of curriculum planning would ask four questions:

1   What kind of society already exists?
2   In what ways is it developing?
3   How do its members appear to want it to develop?
4   What kinds of values and principles will be involved in deciding on this development, as well as the educational means of achieving it?

In the process of cultural analysis it is helpful to view culture as an historical as well as a contemporary phenomenon: not only to take a snapshot of culture now, but also to see how it has developed. In educational analysis we must look for culture lag and curriculum inertia. There is a tendency for schools to lag behind other aspects of social and cultural change, and for the curriculum to become less relevant. This is not to fall into the trap of identifying educational needs with technological advance, nor to equate education with vocational training;

but it is important to recognise that there is a tendency for curricula to get out of date unless efforts are made to counter the natural conservatism of schools.

A selection from the culture is made by analysing society and mapping the kind of knowledge and experiences that are appropriate for the desirable development of that society. Three kinds of classification are needed: first, deciding on major parameters – the cultural invariants or human universals; second, outlining a method of analysis to describe any society making use of those parameters – that is, moving from cultural invariants to cultural variables; third, a means of classifying the educationally desirable knowledge and experiences.

This is to depart from one approach to curriculum planning whereby much discussion took place about the classification of *knowledge* (for example Hirst, 1975) but little attention was paid to the analysis of *society* and deriving from that analysis the kind of knowledge and experiences needed by the young at various stages.

Figure 1 shows this approach as a series of five sequential targets. As a model – a simplified guide to action – it might be used at any level of curriculum planning: national guidelines, or school-based planning, or by an individual teacher.

1   Universals 2   English culture

        3   Cultural analysis

        4   Selection from culture

        5   Curriculum objectives

Figure 1: *Curriculum – a selection from culture*

Some anthropologists have emphasised differences between societies; others have stressed the essential similarities between all societies. My purpose is to begin the analysis by looking at the characteristics that *all* human beings appear to have in common (human universals) and then to analyse how these are or should be related to education.

Cultural invariants/human universals

Some way of subdividing culture is necessary; there is no self-evident classification which would be superior to all others. Bruner (1971) anticipated similar questions when he discussed curriculum planning. He asked *'What is human about being human? How can we make humans more so?'* His answer, in the context of *Man – A Course of Study*, was a set of five *humani*:

forces which should be central to the curriculum: tool-making, language, social organisation, prolonged childhood, and the urge to explain. This has some similarity with the list I shall propose, except that from an anthropological point of view, Bruner's five headings are too limited – unless 'social organisation' is stretched to include almost everything.

In terms of the task in hand, we need a list which is short enough to be manageable, but long enough to facilitate important distinctions. I have elsewhere suggested using the language of conventional anthropological studies and dividing human universals into nine categories (Lawton, 1989). In analysing cultures, I suggest that we focus on nine major headings describing groups of cultural universals. It is not suggested that the nine sub-systems are exhaustive: culture could be sub-classified in a variety of ways. But there are good reasons for suggesting that no society could exist if it lacked any one of the following nine systems, although it might be the case that some of them are more important than others in industrial societies from the point of view of formal education. In other words, a *society* could not exist without any one of the nine, but it is possible to imagine an *education* service without one of them, provided that those experiences were acquired by other means.

The nine cultural invariants or sub-systems are as follows:

1   **Socio-political** system
2   **Economic** system
3   **Communications** system
4   **Rationality** system
5   **Technology** system
6   **Morality** system
7   **Belief** system
8   **Aesthetic** system
9   **Maturation** system.

1   *Socio-political system*

All societies have some kind of social structure – a system of defining relationships within a society. Kinship, status, role, duty and obligation are some of the key concepts. In some societies the social structure is simple, stable and taken for granted; in others it is complex, changing and open to question. The socio-political system tends to be closely related to economic and technological factors: when Western European societies were largely agricultural, the dominant political factor was possession of land; but as trade and industry developed, land ownership became less important than the ownership of the means of production.

2   Economic system

Every society has some means of dealing with the problem of scarce resources, their distribution and exchange, ranging from the very simple to the extremely complex. In simple pre-industrial societies the economic system will tend to be generally understood, but in complex, industrial capitalist societies, many adults may have only a very hazy idea about their own economic system and how it works.

3   Communications system

One of the most significant differences between humans and other animals is the ability to communicate. Communication is by no means absent in other animals, but even the most sophisticated animal systems are crude compared with human communication – especially the ability to communicate by means of language. In those societies where language is entirely spoken, children can learn to develop the communication skills they need informally, simply by interaction with parents and others. In pre-literate societies age, experience and 'memory' are more valued. As writing – and later, printing – develop, the priorities change and specialist forms of knowledge become available to some. But communication consists of more than language: signs, symbols and signalling systems have to be learned by each generation.

4   Rationality system

All societies are rational in the sense of having rules about what is reasonable and what is acceptable as an explanation. The kinds of explanation will differ from time to time and from place to place, but attempts are always made to explain the environment of humans in it. In sixteenth century Europe it was still regarded as rational to explain some events in terms of witchcraft; in some parts of the world it still is. Levi-Strauss (1966) classified societies as 'hot' societies characterised by scientific thinking and 'cold' (primitive) societies which are 'time-suppressing' and rely on myth rather than science and history to explain their world.

5   Technology system

Many writers (including Bruner) have referred to human beings as tool-using and tool-making animals. Recent studies of chimpanzees and other primates show that they too use and make tools of a simple kind, but hardly on a scale deserving the word 'technology'. The process of learning to use tools is always an important feature of human cultures. The system of technology will range from the simple, where every member of society can master the whole of the technology, to the very complex, where no one individual can understand all of it. Specialisation is an economic advantage but aggravates the problem of differential access to knowledge. Modern society may become divided into those who master computerised information retrieval and those who lack the skills to find out.

6   Morality system

Human beings are moral animals, in the sense that all societies have some code of behaviour and make distinctions between right and wrong. What is regarded as appropriate in one society may be different from the rules operating in another place or at another time. In some societies the moral code is unitary and taken for granted; in others, there is value pluralism and the problem of transmitting morality to the young becomes more difficult.

7   Belief system

Every society has a dominant belief system. In some it will be religious, perhaps based on divine revelation. In others, beliefs may be derived from creation myths. In the West, religious beliefs have tended to become weaker, but have not disappeared. Societies are referred to as 'secularised', where 'man is the measure of all things' and scientific explanations occupy a dominant position. There are close connections between the belief system, the morality system and the rationality system.

8   Aesthetic system

All human beings have aesthetic drives and needs. Every society produces some kind of art, even those close to subsistence level. If a society makes cooking pots they will probably decorate them, and standards of excellence will develop.

9   Maturation system

Bruner specified our long childhood as one of the 'humanising forces'. Every society has a set of customs and conventions concerned with growing up. Anthropologists have written extensively on the variety of child-rearing practices which exist. Growth, maturity and ageing are treated differently in various societies, but there are always important customs to be observed. In some developed industrial societies, the problems of transition may be great, partly because there are no clear stages and no clear rules to be applied. With the growth of industrialisation and urbanisation, state agencies, including schools, have taken over some of the functions of the family.

Summary

I have attempted to analyse those characteristics which all human societies have in common. Any human group not possessing each one of those nine systems could not be considered to be a society. No anthropologist has ever found a group of human beings living permanently together which lacked any one of those nine systems.

A society must not only possess the nine systems, but also have some means of *transmitting* them from one generation to the next. Some societies will achieve this cultural transmission partly by means of formal education: if so, a curriculum will be needed. It will be the responsibility of schools to pass on those aspects of culture, unless there are other agencies responsible – curriculum planning is essential.

The argument is deliberately circular: if curriculum is defined as a selection from culture, then the selection must be adequate; culture can be subdivided into nine systems; an adequate selection will include all nine unless we can be assured that the necessary transmission takes place outside schooling.

In this chapter we have been asking very general questions about education, human beings and culture. In Chapter 4, we shall look more specifically at England at the end of the twentieth century as a basis for cultural analysis, and as the beginning of a process of curriculum planning. Teachers must be involved in this process, but teacher professionalism does not mean that they have a monopoly in the field of curriculum planning, which ought to be a democratic arrangement with teachers cast in the key role of converting the school-based design (which they have participated in) into a set of learning schemes and lesson plans.

4

Teachers, cultural analysis and school-based curriculum planning

In Chapter 3 curriculum was defined as a selection from culture; and culture was subdivided into nine cultural systems. I now apply each of the nine systems to contemporary England. Comparisons will also be made between what exists in the culture and what is reflected (and omitted) in the national curriculum.

I also want to introduce another feature of cultural analysis. In the course of analysing contemporary English culture and comparing it with school curricula, some cultural contradictions will be noted. These contradictions are important not only for social reasons, but for their curricular implications. For example, the idea of equality of opportunity is contradicted by the continued existence of the privilege of buying access to certain kinds of education. The study of cultural contradictions has not yet received enough attention from the educational point of view. Tawney (1931) referred to social justice and class in England; some writers have referred to hypocrisy; Edmund King (1979) referred to paradoxes. These are features of many societies, but several writers have drawn attention to the stark cultural contradictions in England. As well as contradictions, attention will be drawn to gaps in the curriculum, and to mismatches identified by the cultural analysis.

It is hoped that the process of cultural analysis will provide some guidance to the task of converting the national curriculum into a whole curriculum. Where a foundation subject coincides with or overlaps one of the cultural systems, the transition from national curriculum to the school-based curriculum will be simplified; but more will need to be said wherever serious gaps are identified.

1   Socio-political system

What kind of society is England at the end of the twentieth century? What should young people learn about that society?

Many volumes have been written about the English social structure and its political system. The following account is only a brief summary.

England is a densely populated, urban industrial society with growing · problems of social control: crime, juvenile delinquency, vandalism and general unrest among the young are on the increase. The problem of coping with young people growing up in an industrial society, especially in overcrowded inner cities, has been seriously underestimated. In recent years there have been additional difficulties in accommodating immigrant minorities, resulting in a series of crises – social, political and educational as well as economic.

An important factor complicating the problem is social class. Class influences and tends to dominate other aspects of life, including education and industry. The 'old boy network' is more powerful in England than in Japan, Germany or the USA. Despite the fact that the class structure has retained feudal vestiges such as the monarchy, the House of Lords, titles and honours, England claims to be a democratic and open society. This is one of the cultural contradictions referred to at the beginning of this chapter. Ideals such as equal opportunity are enshrined in legislation, but the ideal is far from the reality.

England is a complex society with a very elaborate political and social structure. But most young people leave school almost entirely ignorant of the socio-political system. England is an industrialised society, but education has failed to enable many of the young to live harmoniously within that society. They have an imperfect understanding of industrialisation; increasingly they are not educated in such a way as to gain employment or even to cope with unemployment. England is a democratic society with a high rate of social mobility, but schools tend to divide the young socially, academically and culturally, rather than to encourage cooperation, social harmony and a common culture.

These are a few of the contradictions connected with the socio-political system which overlap with some of the other systems. As well as indicating contradictions, any comparison of contemporary culture with the school curriculum will show up gaps and mismatches. Part of the gap-filling exercise would be to recommend that no secondary curriculum should be regarded as satisfactory unless it contained time devoted to social sciences, including political literacy.

Soon after the national curriculum was established, the National Curriculum Council (NCC) accepted the criticism that the ten-foundation-subject approach left serious gaps. To counter the criticism that the national curriculum was inadequate because many important aspects of development and experience were not covered by the foundation subjects, the National Curriculum Council produced *NCC Circular No. 6: The National Curriculum and Whole Curriculum Planning* (NCC, November 1989). It recommended that every school should plan its whole curriculum bearing in mind *cross-curricular* dimensions, themes and skills. This document was followed by more specific suggestions. *Curriculum Guidance 8: Education for Citizenship (NCC, 1990)* offered *'guidance on ways in which education for citizenship might be strengthened and ensured in every school'* (the other four cross-curricular themes were economic understanding, health education, careers, and the environment).

Education for Citizenship was criticised by many for its bland and unchallenging approach; it was also non-statutory and therefore inevitably low priority for many schools. Nevertheless, it could have been a step in the right direction. The curriculum design was based on a classification of objectives under four headings: Knowledge and Understanding, Cross-Curricular Skills, Attitudes, and Moral Codes and Values. These were subdivided as follows:

Knowledge and Understanding:
- The nature of community;
- Roles and relationships in a democratic society;
- The nature and basis of duties, responsibilities and rights.

Cross-Curricular Skills:
- Communication;
- Numeracy;
- Study skills;
- Problem-solving;
- Personal and social;
- Information technology.

Attitudes:
- Independence of thought;
- An enterprising and persistent approach;
- A sense of fair play, including respect for the law and rights of others;
- Respect for different ways of life, beliefs, opinions and ideas;
- A willingness to respect the legitimate interests of others;

Attitudes continued:

- Respect for rational argument and non-violent ways of resolving conflict;
- A constructive interest in community affairs;
- An active concern for human rights;
- Appreciation of the paramount importance of democratic decision-making.

Moral Codes and Values:

- Compare values and beliefs held by themselves and others and identify common ground;
- Examine evidence and opinions and form conclusions;
- Discuss differences and resolve conflict;
- Discuss and consider solutions to moral dilemmas, personal and social;
- Appreciate that distinguishing between right and wrong is not always straightforward;
- Appreciate that the individual's values, beliefs and moral codes change over time and are influenced by personal experience.

Education for Citizenship also made some specific suggestions about the curriculum content that could be used to reach the objectives listed above, stressing that the eight components were interrelated and should not be considered in isolation when planning curriculum provision:

Content: The Essential Components
Three broad areas:

- The nature of community;
- Roles and relationships in a pluralist society;
- The duties, responsibilities and rights of being a citizen.

Five specific contexts:

- The family;
- Democracy in action;
- The citizen and the law;
- Work, employment and leisure;
- Public services.

I do not propose submitting all of *Education for Citizenship* to critical scrutiny – not least because it was never implemented. Secretaries of State from Kenneth Clarke onwards discouraged any further discussion of cross-curricular work, and when the national curriculum ran into serious difficulties in 1993, the Dearing Review was concerned to prune, not to introduce new priorities. The Dearing defence against pressure groups was the doctrine that the national curriculum was not the whole curriculum, and the whole curriculum should be the responsibility of individual schools, not of the School Curriculum and Assessment Authority (SCAA).

Pre-Dearing research by my colleague Professor Geoff Whitty (1994) showed that little work was going on for any of the cross-curricular themes, and Citizenship Education was probably the most neglected:

> It is difficult to see how themes can recover from their present position of having been marginalised by the national curriculum subject orders unless those orders, and the modes of assessment associated with them, are substantially revised. At present, there is no official encouragement to schools to give greater priority to the themes.

2   Economic system

What is the economic system and what should young people know about it?

England is an industrialised society experiencing great difficulty in retaining its place among the most developed and prosperous nations. It relies heavily on the ability to export in order to pay for imports. Only about one-third of food is home-grown.

England was the first country to experience the Industrial Revolution. This gave us economic advantages in the eighteenth and nineteenth centuries which have now become disadvantages. Other countries have learned the lessons of later phases of industrialisation more easily than England, which is handicapped by its pre-industrial social structure and attitudes (Barnett, 1986). In addition, England faced the difficulty of ceasing to be an imperial power, with captive markets and easy sources of cheap raw materials.

One striking feature of English society is that it no longer finds it simple to earn a living: imports exceed exports, despite the great contribution made by service industries, banking, insurance and other 'invisible' exports. Unemployment is high despite a shortage of skilled labour. Finegold and Soskice (1988) have warned us about the danger of what they describe as 'low skills equilibrium', i.e. a society with a citizenry which is under-educated, and a workforce that is poorly trained and whose only merit is that they are cheap – they must therefore be employed on tasks involving little skill and low value-added. Sir Geoffrey Holland (1996) drew attention to this problem in his presidential address to the North of England Educational Conference:

● Last year's World Competitiveness Report from the World Economic Forum shows the UK in 18th place in global competitiveness terms, down from 14th place a year earlier. We come behind the United States, just about every country in Northern Europe, and some of the Pacific rim – Singapore, Japan, New Zealand, Taiwan and Australia. There are many things going for this country. The World Economic Forum rates us the second most competitive country in terms of both foreign direct investment into this country by overseas companies and overseas investment by UK companies. But it is the quality of our workforce and the quality of our education system that let us down. The workforce this year slipped to 24th place in the world in terms of skills, down from 21st place a year earlier. And what the Forum describes as our 'inadequate education system' ranks 35th in the world despite our being at mid-table point (considerably above 35th) in terms both of funding for education and class size in schools ...

● The proportion of the workforce having a university degree is about the same in Britain, France, Germany, the Netherlands and Switzerland. But the proportion holding intermediate level qualifications tells a very different story. In France it is 40%; in Germany 63%; in the Netherlands 57%; in Switzerland 66%. In this country the figure is 25%. The proportion of the workforce having no vocational qualifications is the obverse of that coin: in France 53%; in Germany 26%; in the Netherlands 35%; in Switzerland 23%. In this country the figure is 64%. All this shows through in productivity – and thus in competitiveness. Sooner or later that shows through in jobs, in unemployment, in the economic and social well-being of the country.

Another feature is that England is a capitalist system which has succeeded in withstanding many of the advances of welfare state socialism and, in recent years, recovering some of the lost ground by encouraging programmes of privatisation. The English version of a mixed economy combined with multi-national capitalism, allows a good deal of wealth and power to remain within the control of the ruling class. Many attempts have been made to characterise this aspect of England in the 1990s: for example, Will Hutton (1995) *The State We Are In;* and Hampden-Turner and Trompenaars (1993) *The Seven Cultures of Capitalism.*

There are two major educational implications emerging from this analysis. The first is the need for the young to *understand* the economic system; the second is that the curriculum should enable school-leavers to *take part* in the world of work.

A major educational problem is to define what all young people need to know about their economic system, and then to find time to make this knowledge available to all pupils, in a way which avoids accusations of distortion, bias and even indoctrination. This is difficult, because what needs to be learned includes questions of attitudes as well as knowledge, and the national curriculum was unfortunately framed without including a social science dimension: the opportunity of including economic understanding in the national curriculum for all pupils was missed.

Professor Linda Thomas (in Lawton, 1986) outlined a very useful approach to this problem using the term *economic literacy*. Later, she and Professor Steve Hodkinson elaborated this approach, preferring the title *economic awareness* in a series of publications for the Economic Awareness Teacher Training Programme (EcATT), a partnership between universities, industry, research trusts, central and local government, established in 1986:

> ❝ Young people's experiences of the economic system come from many sources. The media is a major one bombarding them with information and conclusions. Activities such as shopping, choosing, giving, contributing, building, throwing away, working, making, allocating time and resources, sharing, selling and seeing people in need provide experiences in a range of contexts. As a result young people develop an intuitive feel for the economic system - their own commonsense rules. Their behaviour, what they do, how they act and the decisions they make are then influenced, even determined by those perceptions or knowledge. It is possible to become skilled at operating in this way to appear to develop a degree of confidence as certain courses of action are reinforced. It is equally possible to become a pawn, controlled by, rather than in control of, the system. In neither case is true understanding achieved. (Hodkinson and Thomas, 1991)

3   Communications system

The English language is a very important part of the school curriculum, but language is not the only form of communication. A scientific industrialised society uses mathematics; in a democratic society, much information is communicated by statistical charts and diagrams. It is now generally accepted that everyone should become computer literate. And many symbols and signs have to be used – for example, complex systems of road signs.

The division of labour, combined with the development of printing, produced specialised vocabularies and other linguistic features which may make communication difficult. The existence of the mass media is also an important feature of the communication system.

English language is taken seriously as a school subject but is often taught in a limited way from the point of view of the communication system. Reports from the 1920s to the Bullock Report (DES, 1975), the Kingman Report (DES, 1988) and the Cox Report (DES, 1989) have diagnosed shortcomings in the teaching of English. Two points need to be stressed: first, the comparative neglect of *oral* language; second, the failure in many schools to develop a policy of language *across the curriculum*. Many schools also have not yet embarked upon serious planning of programmes to deal with non-linguistic communication. There are many curriculum gaps to be filled. Adequate education in communication would include such topics as film and television studies, advertising techniques and some basic principles of semiotics. Although communication is weightily represented in the national curriculum, many teachers of English and experts on English such as Brian Cox have not been convinced by the 1995 version of the English curriculum (see Cox, 1995).

4 Rationality system

In the terminology used by Levi-Strauss, England is a 'hot' culture. It has coped with rapid social and technological change and has developed a rationality which not only explains change but regards change as normal. This kind of rationality is associated with the Protestant Reformation of the sixteenth and seventeenth centuries which questioned traditional authority and explained the universe 'rationally'. Newtonian science provided a rule system to explain the physical universe; the economics of Adam Smith and the utilitarian philosophy of Bentham and Mill attempted to provide an equivalent scientific method to apply to human behaviour. In England, the scientific form of rationality has become dominant despite doubts about its applicability in the social sciences, and the existence of other kinds of explanation in aesthetics and in other kinds of human experience.

The school curriculum now has to include science, but many children learn science without understanding scientific method and scientific reasoning; and pupils are rarely taught to distinguish the kind of reasoning in science from what would be appropriate in poetry, music or art. Many leave school guilty of 'scientism' – that is, believing that scientific explanation is the only valid form of reasoning. One function of a balanced curriculum will be to illustrate what science can and cannot do. This is not helped by a 'science versus arts' ethos which still characterises some secondary schools; planning the whole curri~ should see different subjects, different forms of know~ cultural systems, as complementary rather than com~

Gareth Morgan (1993) makes the point very nicely

❛ Modern organisations are sustained by belief systems that emphasise the importance of rationality. Their legitimacy in the public eye often depends on their ability to demonstrate rationality and objectivity in action. It is for this reason that anthropologists often refer to rationality as the myth of modern society. For like primitive myth, it provides us with a comprehensive frame of reference or structure of belief, through which we can make day-to-day experience intelligible. The myth of rationality helps us to see certain patterns of action as legitimate, credible, and normal, and hence to avoid the wrangling and debate that would arise if we were to recognise the basic uncertainty and ambiguity underlying many of our values and action.

5   Technology system

In modern society, technology is so complex that no individual can master the whole of it. Specialisation is inevitable. This is an advantage in some respects, but creates the problem of differential access to knowledge. Society may become dangerously divided into those who can master computerised techniques of information retrieval, and those who do not know how to find out. Technology is closely related to the economic system: it is important to develop a good relationship between education, work and technology.

Technology, since 1988, has been part of the compulsory curriculum. But it has been very difficult to define it for schools. There was a great deal of acrimonious debate about the kind of 'Mickey Mouse' school technology involving making things out of toilet-roll cores and egg boxes. At first it was thought possible to include aspects of Home Economics in the technology curriculum, and Domestic Science was elevated to *Food Technology* and Needlework became *Textile Design*. Before that kind of technology was really given a chance to settle down, the critical voices were allowed to prevail and the technology curriculum was completely rewritten.

The post-Dearing technology curriculum, renamed *Design and Technology,* has now been specified and will last at least five years (from 1995). Design and Technology still includes some aspects of Information Technology, but IT has also been increasingly seen as a set of cross-curricular skills, and, in addition, the requirements for IT are now set out separately within the national curriculum as 'Information Technology Capability', with its own set of Programmes of Study and Level Descriptions from Key Stage 1 to Key Stage 4. Design and Technology now concentrates on 'Designing' and 'Making' (the titles of the two Attainment Targets), and there has been a move away from the ❜ne economics' kind of design and making to Design Technology,

Electronics and Control Systems. It is interesting that some attention has been paid to concern for the environment: for example, the Programme of Study for Key Stage 4 includes *'to recognise that moral, economic, social, cultural and environmental issues make conflicting demands ...'.*

Design and Technology remains a difficult subject for primary schools, and secondary schools still face the problem of recruiting sufficiently well qualified teachers for Key Stages 3 and 4. Schools will have the task of deciding whether the new national curriculum is adequate as their whole curriculum, or whether it needs to be supplemented, perhaps by integrating work on the environment and social and moral education.

6   Morality system

England is an example of moral pluralism in which a largely secular morality is dominant. It would be difficult to regard England as a Christian society, despite the continued existence of an Established Church and the assumption made in the 1944 Education Act that religion means Christianity. Since the Reformation, the idea of a single, uncontroversial moral system has been progressively weakened: the Church split into a number of denominations and sects; the whole notion of religious and moral authority was questioned. By the late nineteenth century, a mixture of utilitarian and Christian principles provided the main basis for moral thinking, but the two were often in opposition – another example of cultural contradiction. In the twentieth century, especially after World War Two, immigration from non-Christian societies further complicated the scene. Another difficulty is that *law* and *morality* are often seen as separate: a related danger is what Durkheim referred to as *anomie* – not knowing what the rules of society are. A connected danger is moral relativism – the idea that morality is simply a matter of taste or that one moral code is just as good as any other.

The absence of systematic teaching about the morality system is perhaps the most serious gap in the curriculum. Little attempt has been made to teach elementary ethics, as Dearden (1968) recommended, and few schools have a programme to develop moral autonomy.

Some schools and LEAs have made more progress than others. Some have encouraged the use of tutor-group time for the discussion of practical moral questions along the lines advocated by Button (1981,1982). It will also be necessary for schools to discuss what contributions subjects such as English and history make to moral development. Pring (1984) has also advocated that schools should consciously attempt to become better examples of moral institutions. More so than any of the other cultural systems, the morality system is not only concerned with the curriculum but with the total organisation of the school. But the curriculum cannot be ignored. Pring (1984), at the end of his excellent book, reached the following conclusions which could provide a useful basis for school-based planning:

1. Although there are elements within the content of timetabled subjects which make a valuable contribution to personal development, it would be wrong to identify personal and social education with any subject ...
2. The school, therefore, should start by examining the effect of the school and the curriculum as a whole upon young persons – upon their sense of personal worth ... self-confidence and sense of achievement ... This, of course, requires close attention to what we mean by respecting them as persons ...
3. There is, however, a developmental aspect to this growth as a person – a slow but definite change in the quality of how young people see things from another's point of view, how they reason about matters of moral concern, how they understand and operate within a system of rules ...
4. We need, therefore, to attend in particular to the social and institutional setting which enhances or discourages these various lines of development ... For Kohlberg, 'just communities' were a prerequisite for getting people to take seriously principles of justice in their daily behaviour ...
5. We might extend these more general points about institutional authority to the relationships and the ethos or atmosphere of individual classrooms ... Teaching methods in any subject have their hidden values.
6. ... Concern for the moral behaviour of individuals requires equal concern for the moral atmosphere of the institutions to which they belong ...
7. ... Personal development has its political aspect – even if confined to its development of the capacity to think, to criticise and not to accept injustices lying down. There is a need ... for teachers to be ever more vigilant of the gradual destruction, in the increasingly pragmatic and utilitarian approach to education, of those humanistic values which have, through literature and the arts, been central to our educational tradition.
8. Despite the overriding emphasis upon values that permeate the life of the school as a whole, in particular the way in which authority is exercised, there is a need to respect, too, the need for learning specific concepts, attitudes, abilities, and habits, and the place for this will be through normal timetabled subjects. None the less, this requires, first, coordination of the different subject contributions and secondly, reappraisal within the subjects of their content and method.

Edwin Cox (in Lawton, 1986) made a very interesting contribution to this area of the curriculum. He also quoted with approval a cross-curricular approach developed by Nottingham and Cross (1981), *Moral*

Education Across the Curriculum. In its questions to be answered in devising a curriculum, the Paper highlights the following:

❝ 1.   Does the school:
1.1   Express in its aims its responsibility for the moral development of its pupils?
1.2   Develop a curriculum which:
- offers concrete opportunities for making decisions and acting on them?
- exposes pupils to situations in which their contribution is necessary to the success of the venture or project?
- fosters their self-image without inflating their egos?
- minimises the pressure of compulsion?
- enables pupils to develop independently of their peers without losing involvement with their peers?
- provides for the maximum interaction between pupils and teachers?
1.3   Offer library and other resources which reflect the moral concerns of teachers, pupils and school subjects?
1.4   Encourage in-service training?...
1.5   Define clearly the relationships between pastoral care, careers guidance, health education and moral education?
2   How does each curriculum area relate to the above questions?...
3   What particular contributions can be made by individual subjects?

(quoted by Cox, 1986)

More recently, the School Curriculum and Assessment Authority (SCAA) has returned to the question of moral education in *Spiritual and Moral Development* (SCAA Discussion Paper No.3, September 1995):

❝ Moral development ... cannot be defined by one simple statement. It involves several elements.

- **The will to behave morally as a point of principle** – This attitude is fundamental to moral development.
- **Knowledge of the codes and conventions of conduct agreed by society** – both non-statutory and those prescribed by law.
- **Knowledge and understanding of the criteria put forward as a basis for making responsible judgements on moral issues.**
- **The ability to make judgements on moral issues** – as they arise by applying moral principles, insights and reasoning.

The pamphlet includes some interesting ideas, which could serve as a basis for staff discussions on their school-based curriculum. In any case, all schools will wish to take note of the following 'inspection criteria' (for spiritual and moral development), even if they might appear to be somewhat simplistic:

● Inspection arrangements vary across different types of school ... Schools should evaluate the curriculum and other areas of school life to ensure that appropriate opportunities for spiritual and moral development are being provided. While it is inappropriate for inspectors to make a judgement on the state of individual pupils' spiritual and moral development, it is reasonable to expect teachers and pupils to come to an agreement in the context of records of achievement.

● OFSTED inspects and evaluates schools' provision for spiritual and moral development and pupils' response to this provision. Evidence of such provision is gathered through:

- ■ discussion with the head, other members of staff, and if possible with the Chair of governors;
- ■ observation of lessons and other aspects of the school's work;
- ■ observation of daily collective worship.

● These discussions and observations should indicate whether the school, for example:

- ■ has an agreed approach to the ways in which spiritual and moral issues should be addressed throughout the school;
- ■ promotes an ethos which values imagination, inspiration, contemplation, and a clear understanding of right and wrong;
- ■ offers opportunities in the curriculum for reflective and aesthetic experience and the discussion of questions about meaning and purpose;
- ■ makes adequate provision of Religious Education and collective worship.

7   Belief system

In some ways the problems of the belief system are similar to those of the moral system. There is a lack of consensus, together with dangers of relativism and anomie. Several studies have shown, however, that there is an underlying set of beliefs shared by the vast majority of the population. The belief system is a complex mixture of religious, political and scientific beliefs and values: but contradictions abound.

It has sometimes been suggested that beliefs and values should be transmitted by the family rather than by the school. But it is because there are differences within society between families, and other social groups have a responsibility for dealing with the task from a broader point of view. In many cases, if values and beliefs are not transmitted by the school, they will not be transmitted at all.

There are some ideas and concepts, such as democracy, which tend to be believed in without being understood. Schools need to work out better programmes for developing such values and beliefs, including some opportunities to practise them. It is easier to teach the idea of tolerance than to teach the young to be more tolerant; it is even more difficult to reach agreement on the limits of toleration: in a democracy, at what point should we cease to tolerate those who abuse tolerance and threaten the survival of democracy?

Schools have the task of mapping out the conceptual territory and the related experiences as curriculum objectives. They have to find out the extent to which they will be covered within existing subjects, and, having identified the gaps, make sure the coverage is completed. (Some suggestions have been made in paragraphs 1: socio-political and 6: morality, above.)

8   Aesthetic system

The aesthetic system also presents problems. In the historic process of art being separated from religion, it was also separated from the everyday life of most people. This gave rise to a number of difficulties, made more acute as society became more pluralistic. What counts as art is one problem; and also what counts as *good* art. At a time of rapid social and technological change, the criteria become blurred – and sometimes appear to have been abandoned. Problems of the aesthetic system are related to problems and contradictions within the social structure. What is classified as art tends to be related to the high culture of the upper and upper-middle classes. Art correspondents rarely discuss the aesthetic qualities of cars or furniture; high culture and popular culture are falsely separated.

Teachers are often unclear about high culture and mass culture and uneasy about making judgements about taste. Attempts need to be made to clarify what the issues are in terms of aesthetic criteria and judging what is excellent. The national curriculum goes some way in that direction – but probably not far enough for many schools. Many teachers regret the decision to reduce the status of all aesthetic subjects to that of options (the failure of curriculum planning which was criticised by the HMI Secondary Survey – DES, 1979). Schools will want to ensure that all children have an entitlement to at least some aesthetic experiences 14–16.

9   Maturation system

In England there is some agreement about how babies should be treated, but much disagreement about the extent to which young children should be indulged or encouraged to conform. Habits have changed and are still changing. The Victorian values of 'spare the rod and spoil the child' have given way to greater permissiveness, but experts as well as parents are unsure about some aspects of child rearing.

In England there is no clear-cut demarcation between child and adult; we have a long period of adolescence clouded with doubts and uncertainties. These ambiguities are made worse by legal definitions which are themselves confusing – different ages for marrying, voting, driving a car and so on.

Play and sport are important. The young are expected to play as part of their natural development; older children take part in organised games; adults are expected to take an interest in sport and preferably to participate. But there are regional as well as social class variations.

It is part of the function of education to sort out as much of the confusion as possible, as well as to develop 'healthy' maturation. With the growth of industrial society, various state agencies have taken over some of the functions of the family, especially in health care and child rearing. There are demands to extend schooling downwards to age three or four, partly to enable young mothers to work. At a later stage of maturation, it can no longer be assumed that boys and girls will learn about child rearing in their own families. It is often suggested that 'parenting' needs to be taught in schools as part of the curriculum. But even health education and sex education are inadequately represented in the national curriculum.

School curriculum planning will need to ensure that some adequate coverage of moral education, the belief system and the maturational system is catered for. Before 1988, more and more schools were including personal and social education as a timetabled entitlement rather than as something that form tutors could handle in their spare time. Unfortunately, OFSTED inspectors often complain that PSE lessons are of poor quality. Clearly, some teachers need professional development in this area. But schools also need to establish clear policies which can be reviewed and discussed.

Summary

In this chapter I have taken the process of cultural analysis a little further, in order to show what should be included in a national curriculum and the whole curriculum. I suggest that the national curriculum is deficient in two ways: some cultural systems are missing completely (or almost completely) – for example, the socio-political; second, others are inadequately represented by the foundation subjects. Even if we take into account the NCC cross-curricular themes, there are still gaps. What schools might do about this will be taken up in Chapter 8.

We now have a good deal of information necessary for planning a curriculum in England. But before proceeding to further work on transforming the national curriculum into a school-based whole curriculum, it will be useful to review, separately in Chapters 5 and 6, some recent work on primary and secondary schooling, respectively.

5

The national curriculum and the whole primary experience

Part of the history of primary education in England has been the tension, sometimes open conflict, between those who had a rich vision of what education ought to mean for young children, and those who wanted to impose a narrow, restrictive curriculum and test it by means which further limited the learning process. It would be unfair to see the national curriculum entirely in that light (although there is an element of truth in it). Before the national curriculum there is some evidence from HMI Reports (for example, *The Primary Survey*, DES, 1978) that children in some primary schools were experiencing a curriculum which lacked science or history or geography (or even all three). Jim Campbell (1993) described the twenty years before the national curriculum as 'leaden' rather than golden. On the other hand, there were many schools which organised broad and balanced curricula without having those subjects mentioned specifically on the timetable. When discussing primary schools, there is always a danger of over-generalising, even stereotyping.

Since the national curriculum (1988), all primary schools have been required to teach English, mathematics and science (the three 'core subjects') and six other foundation subjects – technology, history, geography, art, music and physical education (as well as religious education, which is mandatory but not part of the *national* curriculum). For some schools this may have encouraged a broader curriculum; for others it may seem more like a straitjacket. On the whole, schools have probably improved their curriculum planning since 1988, but there is also evidence that many primary teachers find the demands of nine subjects at Key Stage 2 unrealistic. Moreover, any primary school which simply relied on *The National Curriculum* (DFE, 1995) and the Programmes of Study for the nine foundation subjects would not have a satisfactory curriculum even in the way set out by OFSTED (*Framework for the Inspection of Schools,* OFSTED, 1994). Why not?

There are at least two reasons. First, since Dearing (1994), it has been clear that the official view has now been confirmed to be that the national curriculum is not the *whole* curriculum – teachers need to identify the missing ingredients. Second, *The National Curriculum* (DFE, 1995) carefully avoided any direction about how the primary curriculum should be organised – or taught. There is no requirement that the nine foundation subjects should be taught in isolation from each other, although there have frequently been strong political steers in the traditional direction. But that aspect of curriculum planning remains the responsibility of the school and its teachers, working together. The *national* curriculum was a top-down imposition, but the *whole* curriculum has to be school-based. Professional planning by the teachers may yet be the best method of empowerment.

There is also no legal requirement for a school to have a School Development Plan (SDP), although there are strong expectations that planning should take place, with or without a formal document. In practice, all primary schools would be well advised to have a plan which includes some details of the curriculum design. This aspect of planning (that is, SDPs) will be continued in Chapter 9.

How should teachers approach the task of planning a whole curriculum? It may be useful to use subjects as a convenient list of content to be covered, but that is not necessarily the best way of designing a primary school curriculum, not least because it would seem that children do not, at that age, think in terms of subjects; to teach routinely in a subject-by-subject way may be counter-productive. Apart from questions about the content of the curriculum and its assessment, the issue of curriculum organisation and the associated issue of teaching method have been the ones causing primary teachers most concern. There are powerful traditions operating within primary education, and it may be helpful to remind ourselves very briefly of some of the episodes in the debate.

Changing perspectives in primary education

The term *primary school* arose out of the discussions of the first Hadow Report, *The Education of the Adolescent* (1926), which recommended a break in elementary education at age eleven:

❝ There is a tide which begins to rise in the veins of youth at the age of eleven or twelve. It is called by the name of adolescence. If that tide can be taken at the flood, and a new voyage begun in the strength and along the flow of its current, we think that it will 'move on to fortune'. We therefore propose that all children should be transferred, at the age of eleven or twelve ...

This recommendation was carried forward to the terms of reference of the second Hadow Committee, which was set up in 1928:

❝ To inquire into and report as to the courses of study suitable for children ... up to the age of eleven in Elementary Schools, with special reference to the needs of children in rural areas.

The Committee's Report, *The Primary School*, was published in 1931. In the Introduction, reference was made to three phases of curriculum which the previous hundred years had witnessed.

First phase:

❝ In the age before the establishment of a public education system, when even some of those who agreed that it was desirable that children should learn to read, 'if only for the best of purposes, that they may read the Scriptures', were doubtful if it was desirable to teach them to write, since 'such a degree of knowledge might produce in them a disrelish for the laborious occupations of life', questions of curriculum were naturally not a burning issue.

Second phase:

❝ In the period immediately preceding and following 1870, the period of the Revised Code (payment by results) and the early school boards, the dominant – and, indeed it is hardly an exaggeration to say, the exclusive concern of most schools was to secure that children acquired a minimum standard of proficiency in reading, writing and arithmetic, subjects in which their attainments were annually assessed by quantitative standards, with a view to the allocation to schools of pecuniary rewards and penalties.

Third phase:

❝ During the last forty years, and with increasing rapidity in the twelve years since 1918, the outlook of the primary schools has been broadened and humanised. Today it includes care, though the school medical service, for the physical welfare of children, offers larger, if still inadequate, opportunities for practical activity, and handles the curriculum not only as consisting of lessons to be mastered, but as providing fields of new and interesting experience to be explored; it appeals less to passive obedience and more to the sympathy, social spirit and imagination of the children, relies less on mass instruction and more on the encouragement of the individual and group work, and treats the school, in short, not as the antithesis of life, but as its complement and commentary.

The section of the report on Curriculum included the famous sentence *'We are of the opinion that the curriculum of the primary school is to be thought of in terms of activity and experience, rather than of knowledge to be acquired and facts to be stored.'* The Report also said: *'The primary school has its own canons of excellence and criteria of success; it must have the courage to stand by them.'* What was true in 1931 still applies today.

Such ideas may seem remarkable for 1931. And two years later there was an equally progressive report on nursery education.

I will resist the temptation to go back further to discuss the influence of Rousseau, Pestalozzi and Froebel, although there is some evidence of those ideas in the Hadow Report – probably indirectly. Closer in time to the Hadow Committee were the writings of John Dewey, who believed in the value of experience and activity: understanding was more important than memorisation. Dewey, unlike Rousseau, stressed the positive aspects of the social environment. He would have agreed on much of the advice on curriculum in the 1931 Report, and would probably have been saddened by the missed opportunities of planning a primary school curriculum in 1988.

One of the influences on Hadow was the New Educational Fellowship (NEF). The NEF, which had existed since the First World War (founded by Edmond Holmes, Percy Nunn, Michael Sadler and others), was a group who disagreed on many issues but were all profoundly dissatisfied with the regimentation and repressive atmosphere of most schools at the time, and became associated with a number of small 'progressive' independent schools. A significant book for the NEF was by the ex-inspector, Edmond Holmes: in *What Is And What Might Be* (1911), Holmes contrasted what he saw as the anti-educational practices of most elementary schools with the very enlightened views of one elementary school headteacher. Holmes claimed that the education generally given to pupils in elementary schools was misguided: teachers were compelled to destroy the freedom, initiative and intelligence of their charges.

Why were elementary schools guilty of the practices that horrified Holmes? We have to remind ourselves that the origins of nineteenth century elementary education were connected with prevailing thinking about factories and industrial training, about discipline and such habits as punctuality and obedience. Holmes was an inspector (or Chief Inspector) for thirty years (1875–1905) and was convinced that the whole system had to be changed. He was hardly typical of HMI at the time, but there were many other HMI who had progressive views and who may have been influenced by him. Selleck (1972) described the period 1902–1944 as 'new education' dominated by progressive ideas. Selleck though' that HMI were partly responsible, showing that their 1927 *Handbook of Suggestions* had moved a long way in the progressive direction since the 1905 edition.

The growth of progressivism was steady but still very slow after 1931: we should not forget that it was not until the 1960s that all 5–11 year olds were in primary schools – let alone progressive schools. It is always dangerous to generalise from personal experience, but I was a pupil in an elementary school junior department (5–11) from 1936–1942 and I can recall very little that could be described as progressive.

The 1944 Education Act officially abolished elementary schools and implemented the Hadow recommendation of moving from primary to secondary school at 11+. Primary education became a reality for nearly all children, but not yet in an enlightened form. Despite the post-war problems, the move away from traditional elementary practice continued. Public endorsement of progressive primary methods had to wait until the Plowden Report (1967). Clearly the Report did not invent child-centred primary education, but it was seen as giving official blessing. Maurice Kogan (1987) was almost certainly correct when he spoke of the Committee's conclusion *'that a strong minority of primary schools were successful in inculcating attitudes and relationships towards pupils that the Hadow Reports of 1931 and 1933 had thought appropriate'*. Some LEAs were more advanced than others – for example, the West Riding of Yorkshire, Oxfordshire and Leicestershire were by now very proud of their progressive primary schools.

What did the Plowden Report advocate? First, it should be recalled that much of the Report is concerned with matters other than teaching method – heredity and environment, social class, Education Priority Areas, the age of transfer, are all discussed at length. Nevertheless, there is almost unquestioning support for child-centred methods of teaching: the child should be happy, should be given work that is of individual interest, and should be active; learning should be based on personal experience. Much of this doctrine was, as we have seen in this chapter, developing steadily throughout the century, largely as a reaction against the repressive methods of the nineteenth century.

The importance of the Plowden Report in encouraging progressive teaching methods is still in dispute. Some talked of the 'Plowden Revolution', others have denied that the Report made much difference. The truth is almost certainly somewhere in between. The Report became accepted as an official point of view on primary education and was used in Colleges of Education as part of the education canon, as well as being source material for INSET courses. It is also clearly the case that as soon as it was published it began to be attacked – partly because it was seen as a further move towards egalitarianism, and partly because the 'Plowden methods' were regarded by some as either impracticable or objectionable in principle. An essential skill for primary teachers in the 1990s is to distinguish between educationally valid aspects of progressive or child-centred education and those which have been rightly dismissed as mere trendiness.

Those who attacked Plowden in principle can be divided into two overlapping groups: first, those who raised philosophical and practical objections, and second, those who objected politically to what they saw as a threat to order and stability. The first group included R. S. Peters and others at the University of London Institute of Education who published *Perspectives on Plowden* (1969); the second group, quite independently, produced the first Black Paper, *Fight for Education* (1969). But there is an overlap: for example, Bantock's Black Paper on 'discovery' methods has been supported by educationists and psychologists.

Peters attacked the Plowden Report for basing some of its recommendations on 'needs' and 'interests'. He claimed that an approach based on such dubious concepts could be dangerous; he also attacked the psychological model of the pupils adopted in the Report.

In the same year (1969) Cox and Dyson produced *Fight for Education*. This Black Paper had originally been intended as a document criticising changes in universities, but Cox and Dyson were persuaded to widen its appeal by condemning progressive primary methods and comprehensive schools. The tone of later Black Papers was more extreme, and some of the Black Paper authors carried the argument over into the popular press. For example, Boyson wrote in the *Daily Telegraph* about William Tyndale School as part of a left-wing conspiracy: *'It is a favourite trick of the extreme left to destroy all values and all morality and to create what Trotsky called "human dust"'* (quoted by Ellis, 1976). This attack was unashamedly ideological, seeking a return to traditions, objecting to child-centred methods which encouraged children to question authority and which exaggerated the value of creativity whilst paying insufficient attention to skills and discipline.

Some of the educationists later moderated their views; the politicians did not. R. S. Peters, just before his retirement, told me that he felt that *Ethics and Education* (1966) and *Perspectives on Plowden* (1968) were not philosophically satisfactory and he wanted to bring back some metaphysics into the philosophy of education. He was no longer convinced that the philosophy of education should be confined to linguistic analysis. His colleague, Paul Hirst, also changed his mind, later but more publicly (see O'Hear and White, 1993). But I doubt if either

Peters or Hirst would want to endorse progressive practices entirely: one of the problems with an orthodoxy (if child-centred education ever was an orthodoxy) is that the apathetic and lazy are tempted to join a movement they do not fully understand. Whilst there were some excellent primary teachers who could produce superb results, there were others who only went through the motions of progressive practice. A good example is the progressive doctrine of 'readiness' – children will learn to read when they are ready, and premature efforts to teach reading will be worse than useless; this is a comfortable doctrine for the idle teacher who sees no need to do anything to stimulate readiness. The growth in popularity of progressive methods had also coincided with the decline of the 11+ examination as a determiner of curriculum and teaching methods: this left some schools in a state of confusion.

One extreme example of such a school was the notorious William Tyndale Primary School in Islington, where a mixture of laziness, incompetence and misinterpreted educational theory on the part of some teachers caused parents to demand change. The Auld Report (1976) condemned the practices which had been allowed to go on for too long. This event was reported with enthusiasm by the popular press, and it was assumed that there were many similar schools waiting to be condemned.

In the same year, 1976, the Prime Minister, James Callaghan, made his famous Ruskin speech which, although more related to secondary schools, called into question the relevance of the curriculum and the appropriateness of teaching methods. The Great Debate raised questions of curriculum control, but the political will to develop a national curriculum was lacking. (For one reason the Schools Council still existed as the professional voice on curriculum matters.)

In 1979 there was a change of government – the beginning of the Thatcher administration. In January 1980 the DES published a document on curriculum clearly intending to put right some of the inadequacies detected after the issue of Circular 14/77. *A Framework for the School Curriculum* (DES, 1980) was a centralist document suggesting not only a subject-based curriculum, but with allocations of time included for each subject. This was attacked by teachers and other educationists for its technicist approach, and it was modified in the following year to become *The School Curriculum* (DES, 1981). This was followed by two more Circulars calling for LEA action on the curriculum: Circular 6/81 and Circular 8/83, each calling the attention of LEAs to their responsibility for curriculum policy and control. LEAs at this time were being instructed to take seriously the task of curriculum planning.

Meanwhile another group were making a bid to exert influence over the curriculum. In the early 1970s the Curriculum Publication Group within HMI were discussing and writing about a common, or entitlement, curriculum. In December 1977 they produced *Curriculum 11–16* (DES, 1977) which contained a curriculum model they were later to develop as a set of guidelines for primary (as well as secondary) schools. A national curriculum of some kind became increasingly likely, but neither of Margaret Thatcher's first two Secretaries of State for Education – Mark Carlisle and Keith Joseph – were enthusiastic, and the initiative planned by some civil servants in the Education Department had to wait until Kenneth Baker took over in 1986.

It was by now quite clear that a national curriculum of some kind would emerge: but would it be a bureaucratic control model favoured by the DES, or the HMI professional, entitlement model being developed and tried out in some schools? In the end it would be decided by the politicians. The losers were professional teachers who after 1988 tended to be treated as employees who had to obey, rather than professionals free to innovate. The 1988 national curriculum imposed a subject-based model on primary schools complete with an over-elaborate testing programme. The details of that fiasco are contained elsewhere in this book.

Suffice to say here that the 1993 teachers' test boycott led to a national curriculum somewhat reduced in detail, but with all the major problems unsolved and still not matching the requirements of the kind of curriculum and teaching methods which had been evolving in the best primary schools since the Hadow Reports of 1931 and 1933. After the Dearing Report in 1993–4 there were further attempts to make teachers adopt traditional methods.

What was this dispute about? Was it simply a question of traditional and progressive ideologies? The answer is quite complex. To some extent there was still a dispute about whether the purpose of education – as discussed in Hadow (1931) – was to encourage passive learning and obedience or enquiry and problem-solving. But even without that ideological difference, there were disputes about the most effective ways of teaching and learning 5–11. The whole debate is complex and cannot be reduced to progressive/traditional or formal/informal dichotomies. (See Galton, 1995, for an excellent discussion of this whole problem.)

It may be useful to group the theoretical issues into *four kinds of change,* despite the fact that they overlap at many points. Some of the classroom implications of the changes may be disputed, but it is clear that the attitude of teachers towards their pupils has changed dramatically since the nineteenth century and continuously during the twentieth century. Teachers now tend to treat their pupils very differently from the elementary school teacher working to the Revised Code (1862) and payment by results.

From tabula rasa *to process*

The teacher's view of the learner has moved away from the idea of an empty vessel to be filled with useful information, or from memorisation of facts or other content items. It has moved towards the understanding of concepts and ideas. The emphasis has changed from learning parts to understanding the whole. The influence of Gestalt psychology should not be underestimated. Gestalt psychology had been developing in Germany since the beginning of the twentieth century. (Gestalt is the German word for 'configuration'.) The main assumption was that the human brain has a tendency to organise experience into patterned configurations or wholes.

This change to holistic learning has sometimes been referred to as *'process'*. In Chapter 2 reference was made to Bruner (1960), who emphasised the importance of teachers themselves becoming knowledgable about the 'structure' of the subject matter they want to teach: knowing what are the *key* ideas and concepts which will enable pupils to understand the subject matter. Teachers must also have regard for *sequence* – the best order of presentation. Clearly, this kind of structured teaching and learning is very different from simply allowing children to discover everything for themselves. There is also a considerable overlap between what Bruner described and what has more recently been discussed as constructivism (see below).

From stages of development to interaction and intervention

Critics of the Plowden Report have sometimes accused it of overemphasising the importance of Piaget, or encouraging oversimplified interpretations of Piaget's stages of development which produced a negative view of children, spelling out what they could not do yet, rather than what was needed to stimulate them. Since Plowden there have been many studies which have modified the views of Piaget (see Donaldson, 1978). On the other hand, Vygotsky (1978) has become more important. Whereas Piaget was essentially a genetic epistemologist (more interested in the development of children's thinking than in teaching), Vygotsky was fundamentally concerned with the process of learning. He said that too much attention was paid to the negative aspects of early stages of development rather than to what children know. One of his key ideas is the 'zone of proximal development' (ZPD), which is concerned with the task of the teacher in encouraging the pupil to go a little beyond what the child already knows. Vygotsky also stressed the importance of language in development – another aspect of learning that Piaget tended to neglect.

Bruner has become a crucial figure in bridging the gap between Piaget and Vygotsky. Bruner talked in terms of three stages – *enactive*, *iconic* and *symbolic*. But he was sceptical of the notion of 'readiness', saying that it was a dangerous half-truth: *'Anything can be taught to any child at any stage of development in some intellectually honest form.'* Bruner saw a much more positive role for the teacher. These developments of the ideas of Piaget, Vygotsky and Bruner are now often referred to as *constructivism*, and should not be dismissed as 'trendy progressivism' although it is not, as yet, a total theory of learning.

Constructivism covers a variety of meanings, but the various authors seem to agree on three important points: (*a*) behaviourist stimulus-response theories of learning are inadequate; (*b*) knowledge cannot be reduced to remembering facts – reflection and interpretation are important; (*c*) teaching is a subtle mixture of understanding the structure of the subject matter, the thinking processes of the child (maybe at a given stage) and the processes of interaction (transactions) between the teacher and student. But we should also note Neville Bennett's (1987) criticism: *'Constructivist models of the child contain no serious treatment of the social environment in which learning takes place.'* Those who claim to avoid these dangers may call themselves 'social constructivists', thus further distancing themselves from Piagetian studies of individual children.

From the class or age-group to the individual

One of the difficulties of primary teaching is for the teacher to move the whole class along in the same direction, whilst recognising that the range of achievement will be considerable. Progression is important, but so is differentiation. Young student teachers are sometimes told that a useful method is to split the class into smaller groups. But to do this effectively is more difficult than first appears: pupils have to be taught how to work in groups, to listen to each other, to work together, to discuss constructively and to reach agreement. Galton (1995) has pointed out from his research that many 'groups' are in fact no more than collections of individuals working alone.

Part of the task for the professional teacher is to plan carefully what kind of learning needs to be individual, what should be learned in a group, and when it would be better to have a whole-class presentation by the teacher, always bearing in mind that pupils benefit from verbal interaction with the teacher. This is a very different picture from children simply engaging in 'activities', either as individuals or in groups. One of the stereotypes of the post-Plowden classroom is that teachers never teach the class as a whole, but set work for groups or individuals, or simply leave them to 'discover'. This is quite untrue, but it *is* true that there has been a sensible move away from treating all children as though they could proceed to learn everything at the same pace.

There is a further complication: part of the teacher's plan should be to cater for different levels of ability. This is very difficult and Neville Bennett (1987) has observed that *'approximately 40% of tasks matched pupils' capabilities, but there was a strong trend towards the over-estimation of low attaining pupils and the under-estimation of high attainers'*. This is a finding supported by HMI evidence (DES, 1978, 1983, 1985). Schools need to have a policy on how to develop teachers' professional skills in this area.

The professional teacher will also bear in mind the fact that children have different learning styles – it is not just a matter, as Piaget seemed to suggest, of providing plenty of concrete examples. The primary classroom will contain about thirty children, who are unique. They must be treated as individuals, yet they must also be taught to learn as a group. This aspect of classroom management is one of the most difficult (see below). But the Plowden doctrine of treating children as individuals can be taken too far. Teachers who set up tasks for individual children have a complex management problem which takes up all their energies (Simon, 1981, quoted by Gipps, 1992).

From intelligence to intelligences

A final change of attitude to the learner concerns the concept *'intelligence'*. In the past, some teachers may have been satisfied with simply classifying children as bright, average or dull, as though intelligence were a single dimension. Recent work in psychology has shown that conventional intelligence tests have concentrated on one very limited form of intelligence and encouraged teachers to ignore many other kinds of intelligent behaviour. In the USA, Howard Gardner (1983) has devoted a great deal of research to the concept of intelligence and now talks of multiple intelligences. He suggests seven kinds of intelligence:

Verbal linguistic
Logical mathematical
Visual spatial
Body kinesthetic
Musical rhythmic
Interpersonal (others)
Intrapersonal (self).

This is a very important theory for professional teachers to discuss. It suggests that not only is the traditional curriculum too narrow in terms of human abilities, but also that we should be looking for abilities and talents in *all* pupils rather than accepting a classification of 'below average'. Professional teachers will have a richer concept of 'ability' than the average parent. Daniel Goleman (1995) has recently complicated the discussion of intelligence still further in his book *Emotional Intelligence*. Goleman suggests that in future the performance of pupils in tests of *emotional maturity* may be considered more important than IQ.

Neither the Dearing Review (1994) nor the recommendations of the 'three wise men' (Alexander, Rose and Woodhead, 1992) solved the problems of the primary school curriculum and the related question of teaching methods. The solution remains in the hands of teachers in individual schools. They should guard against the reactionary views of some politicians and even some educationists (for example Woodhead, 1995).

School development plans need to show clearly *how* teachers intend reaching beyond the national curriculum to develop a professionally planned whole curriculum. The school development plan will also have much to say about the organisation of the curriculum and how this relates to classroom practice. Part of the solution is also for teachers to cease to regard what goes on in 'my classroom' as an individualist, private concern. These points will be taken up again in Chapter 9.

Effective primary teaching

What kind of theory and research knowledge should professional primary teachers have in order to plan, cooperatively, a whole-school curriculum? Clearly the task does not involve a simple choice between progressive and traditional ideologies – the situation is far more complex. My colleague, Caroline Gipps, has fortunately provided some excellent advice in *What We Know About Effective Primary Teaching* (1992). This is a publication which should be read by all primary teachers, especially when they are embarking upon curriculum planning or designing a school development plan. Here I can do no more than highlight a few major points.

Gipps begins by emphasising that Piaget underestimated the role of language whilst overestimating play: one result of this was, as Barbara Tizard (another researcher from the Institute of Education) pointed out, the development of large open-plan nurseries (and primary classrooms) so that children roamed from one activity to another, when what they really needed was sustained conversation with an adult. Another legacy from Piaget was the now very familiar problem of low teacher expectations of primary pupils.

Modifications to Piaget by Bruner (1966) and others led to a more balanced constructivist model of learning which envisages the child as an active agent in her own learning – not (as in the traditional transmission model) as an empty vessel to be filled. The constructivist position is, however, very different from the extreme progressive, curriculum-free model of waiting for the child to be ready to choose what to discover for herself. The constructivist model sees the need for a carefully planned curriculum for the whole class (and whole school) which is sufficiently flexible to cater for individual differences. But the idea of a different curriculum plan for every pupil is a nonsense. Brian Simon (1981) pointed out the fallacy of the interpretation of Plowden which focused on the individual child and saw only individual differences: pedagogy (in a class of 25 or 30) has to start with what the children have in common, whilst not assuming that they are identical. Teachers who try to set up separate tasks for every child on an individual basis give themselves an impossible problem of classroom management and little or no time for productive communication. This was confirmed by Maurice Galton (1987) from the evidence of the ORACLE project. Curriculum planning and pedagogy are closely connected. Galton also demonstrated that teachers who decide to work with individual children were forced to set tasks which did not make many demands on the teacher but relied instead on worksheets or published schemes of doubtful educational value.

But it is not only the *quantity* of communication in the context of a structured curriculum that matters: research consistently shows that high achievement by pupils is related to the *quality* of the teacher's communication – especially her questioning skills. Teachers also need to be sufficiently confident of the subject matter they are teaching to be able to ask higher-order questions rather than those demanding simple yes/no answers or one-word responses. Some teachers are found to restrict their communication almost entirely to routine factual statements or commands. The primary curriculum needs to be planned with the need for good teacher-pupil communication as a very high priority. That will necessarily involve some whole-class teaching, of the kind where high-level questioning is possible, and which encourages sustained interaction between the teacher and the pupils. The alternative – a curriculum designed for individualised work – has the disadvantage of relying too much on impersonal worksheets or assignments where communication is minimal and where it is found that pupils react by slowing down their pace of work.

This does not mean, however, that teachers should spend all their time teaching the whole class: the professional skill lies in knowing when to teach the whole class together and when to split them down into groups or individuals (and to know *why*). A planned, structured curriculum also tends to cut down the amount of time wasted. Tizard (1988) pointed out that in low-achieving classes where teachers had low expectations for their pupils, children spent about half the day at play, 'dinner time' and other non-work activities. A planned curriculum tended not only to have more 'time on-task' but also to consist of a wider range of interesting activities, tackled systematically one by one, but with a variety of tasks available within the curriculum, for the whole range of ability. A common curriculum, or a common assignment within the curriculum, need not be a uniform curriculum. Teachers need a wide range of approaches, as well as familiarity with what research tells us. A final word should go to Caroline Gipps (1992):

So theory's contribution lies in the insights that it can give us: not for any one theory's ability to give us all, or indeed any, of the right answers, but to offer a range of insights which we can use to build up an understanding of the science *and* art of teaching within the complex classroom setting.

It is hoped that those insights will help teachers to face the task of curriculum design more confidently. This discussion will be continued in Chapters 8 and 9.

Summary

The history of primary education has sometimes been expressed as a conflict between traditionalism and progressivism. This is too simple a description to guide teachers in primary schools facing the task of interpreting the national curriculum in the 1990s. Nevertheless, it is possible to describe four aspects of pedagogical change: from seeing the pupil as an empty vessel to be filled, to the idea of a pupil dynamically interacting with new experiences and processes; from simplistic ideas of stages of development, to the role that teachers must play in facilitating pupils' development; from seeing all pupils as needing more or less the same treatment, to treating children as individuals (but preserving whole-class teaching and group work as useful techniques); and finally, from thinking of ability in terms of a single kind of intelligence, to understanding intelligence in a variety of dimensions. All four kinds of pedagogical change are associated with the high priority given to the quality and quantity of communication between teachers and pupils. There is a good deal of theoretical work in this field which teachers need to be familiar with.

6

Secondary education, from ERA to Dearing

In the previous chapter I described the debate on the primary curriculum which has been waged since primary schools first began. Discussions of the secondary curriculum have been similar in some respects, but quite different in others. Understanding the nature of this debate is a prerequisite for appreciating the finer points of some of the argument over the secondary curriculum – including the national curriculum 1988 and the Dearing reforms since 1993. It is, therefore, necessary to go back a little further than 1988.

Selection

At the beginning of this century the discussion of secondary schools centred not on the curriculum but on access to secondary education. The 1902 Education Act made it possible for LEAs to develop County Secondary Schools (grammar schools) and the 1904 Regulations laid down a minimum curriculum. There was no great curriculum debate at the time, since the County Schools simply followed the traditional curriculum which had been developed by Independent Schools, and little controversy was involved. Complaints about the new secondary schooling focused almost entirely on the fact that it was extremely difficult for working-class children to gain admittance; the majority of places in the County Schools were for fee-payers, only a small percentage of 'scholarships' being made available for the brightest pupils in elementary schools to transfer at eleven – the 'ladder of opportunity'.

Attempts were made in the 1930s to argue for fairer methods of selection. For example, Gray and Moshinsky (1938) argued that there were large numbers of highly intelligent working-class pupils who did not get to a grammar school or a university. At this time the argument tended to be about *fairer* selection rather than challenging the principle of selection itself; the National Union of Teachers argued that the 11+ examination should be seen as a *qualifying standard* allowing all who could benefit from secondary education a place, not as a selective or competitive device. Only a few voices in the Labour Party and the TUC talked in terms of a 'broad highway' rather than the 'ladder of opportunity'. After 1944, research took the form of a series of sociological or 'demographic' studies about equality of educational opportunity, focusing on social class.

Meanwhile in 1938 and 1943 there were two official Reports which contributed to the debate about curriculum. The Spens Report (1938) on secondary education with special reference to grammar schools and technical high schools was much influenced by the prevailing psychology of the time – or perhaps by oversimplifications of those views which were dominated by intelligence testing. The result was to reinforce the idea that there were different kinds of *children* – academic, technical and practical – who required different kinds of curriculum; the most likely organisational solution was to have three different types of secondary school – grammar, technical and modern schools. Clearly, such ideas have not yet disappeared from discussions about secondary education.

The Norwood Report (1943) on curriculum and examinations in secondary schools reinforced the Spens segregationist way of thinking about secondary schools, although it was envisaged that there should be a two-year 'diagnostic' period at 11–13 before boys and girls would be finally allocated to an academic, technical or practical destiny. In practice this tripartite system became, in many LEAs, a selective process for either grammar school or modern school: the numbers of technical schools were always small.

Towards comprehensivisation

In the period after World War Two, the major task for both central government and LEAs was ensuring that there were enough teachers and classrooms to cope with the increasing numbers of secondary pupils. The increased numbers resulted from the 1944 Act which made secondary education free and compulsory for all up to age 15 (and later 16); there was also a post-war rise in the birth rate resulting in the 'population bulge' which reached secondary schools in the mid-1950s. The result was tremendous pressure on school building and teacher-training numbers; there was little time for discussion of curriculum, although some schools were more successful than others in breaking away from the elementary tradition.

The 1944 Act had not discussed curriculum. During the war a national curriculum was still thought of as a fascist or totalitarian idea; after 1944 the Ministry of Education left the question to LEAs, who generally regarded it as a matter for schools to determine. In 1957, W. O. Lester Smith was still able to write:

> This tradition of partnership is the outstanding feature of our educational administration. Although we have now endowed the Minister with great power, in practice he and his Ministry of some 3000 officials function as members of a great fellowship – Ministry, Local Authorities, Teachers, Voluntary Associations – friends working together with mutual understanding in a great cause. In 1950 the Ministry celebrated a Jubilee; there had been a unified central department for half a century as a consequence of the Board of Education Act of 1899. The Minister...George Tomlinson and the Permanent Secretary, Sir John Maud, crystallised the story in a joint introduction, and it was this partnership that they singled out as the crowning achievement.

It was, of course, George Tomlinson (Minister of Education 1947–51) who made the famous remark *'Minister's nowt to do with curriculum'*. In the Jubilee publication, Tomlinson also said:

> If this Report comes into the hands of readers from overseas ... they may be expected to look first for a substantial chapter on educational method and the curriculum of the schools. They will not find it ... In all matters affecting the curriculum and methods of teaching it has been content to offer guidance by means of suggestions. (quoted in Lester Smith, 1957)

Curriculum was still seen as a professional not a political matter; and this view was shared by Conservative Ministers until the 1960s. Even the Crowther Report (1959), which was critical of the secondary curriculum, stopped short of suggesting any kind of national curriculum.

How did this tradition change to the rampant interference of the 1980s and 1990s?

One reason was the ever-increasing cost of education. Sooner or later it was likely that questions would be asked about 'value for money', especially when comparisons were made (accurately or otherwise) between educational standards in England and those of our 'competitors'. During the 1970s the word *accountability* was used with increasing frequency in the context of education. But there had been attempts to influence the curriculum much earlier. In 1960, David Eccles (Conservative Minister of Education) said that he regretted that Parliamentary debates on education were so much devoted to bricks and mortar and matters of organisation rather than the content of the curriculum. He said that he intended to make the *'Ministry's voice heard rather more often and positively and no doubt controversially'*. Soon afterwards the Curriculum Study Group was established. Teachers and LEAs were alarmed and opposed the new organisation. In 1963 a new Minister, Sir Edward Boyle, decided to yield to professional pressure and set up the Lockwood Committee, which recommended that the Schools Council for Curriculum and Examinations should be established.

This was different from the Curriculum Study Group in a number of ways, notably by giving teachers a majority on all important Schools Council committees (except the finance committee). Unfortunately, the ideology of the teaching profession at that time was that only teachers had a right to make decisions about the curriculum, and the Schools Council adopted a policy of producing materials for subject teaching (and some examples of inter-disciplinary teaching) but resisted the idea of a centralised curriculum. The opportunity was, therefore, missed of developing a national curriculum which was professional rather than bureaucratic and political.

In the midst of the transition from the Curriculum Study Group (1962) to the Schools Council (1964) there was another Report on some aspects of secondary education – the Newsom Report (1963), which was particularly concerned with the 13–16 age group of pupils 'of average or less than average ability'. The Report began with a topical value-judgment: *'We are concerned that the young people whose education we have been considering should receive a greater share of the national resources devoted to education than they have in the past.'* This was a frank admission that the policy of parity of esteem between grammar and secondary modern schools was simply not working – even in crude financial terms. The Report was concerned to improve the quality of education for *'Half Our Future'*, and urged raising the school leaving age to 16 as soon as possible. The Report failed, however, to generate a plan for the whole curriculum. And although the Report made assumptions about the desirability of increasing social justice, the issue of comprehensive reorganisation and its curricular implications was avoided.

In 1965 the Labour Party made comprehensive secondary schools part of its official policy and issued a Circular (10/65) requesting all LEAs to make plans for secondary reorganisation along comprehensive lines. Partly in reaction to this policy, from about that time there was a sharp division between the two major Parties on education. The first of the

Black Papers appeared in 1969, criticising a policy which would 'destroy' good schools (that is, grammar schools).

There was a change of government in 1970, and Margaret Thatcher became Secretary of State for Education for four years. Nevertheless, the swing to comprehensive schools continued, mainly because, even in Conservative-controlled LEAs, selection at 11+ was seen as undesirable. The DES also appeared to be increasingly concerned about standards, and in 1974 the Assessment of Performance Unit (APU) was set up (see page 81). In 1976 a new Permanent Secretary at the DES, Sir James Hamilton, questioned the lack of attention paid to views of parents and employers, and criticised teachers for sheltering behind their expertise. In 1976, too, suggestions that the curriculum was too important to be left to the teachers came from the political Left as well as the Right. Ann Corbett (1976), in the Fabian Society's evidence to the Taylor Committee, suggested that reformed governing bodies of schools should exercise greater control over the curriculum. On the Right, Tim Raison (1976) said that the 1944 Act's failure to provide guidelines for the curriculum was unfortunate.

1976 was important in other respects. The *10th Report of the Expenditure Committee of the House of Commons* focused attention on the finance of education and the lack of control that the DES had. This Committee was also critical of the fact that the DES had little to say about the curriculum. Towards the end of this year, the Prime Minister, James Callaghan, questioned whether schools were doing enough to produce adequately qualified young people. Many of these complaints could be seen as questions about value for money. In addition, consumerism was beginning to develop in the form of parental demands.

Public examinations

Meanwhile, another aspect of the curriculum debate was proceeding: to some extent the story of secondary education and its curriculum was overshadowed by the changes in public examinations from 1963 onwards. The Certificate of Secondary Education (CSE) had been introduced as an examination for the 40 per cent of pupils below the 20 per cent taking the General Certificate of Education (GCE) O level. This was generally welcomed by teachers and others. CSE differed from GCE O level in many ways: it was more in the hands of teachers themselves, and there was more opportunity for school-based syllabuses to be offered (in the form of Mode 2 and Mode 3 examinations). Coursework was a feature of many syllabuses. The balance had swung away from an emphasis on national standards towards school-based curricula and assessment; how to moderate school-based results to achieve national comparability was a problem yet to be solved. But comparability was seen as a problem partly because grade 1 CSE was regarded as equivalent to a pass (A–C) at O level.

Despite a number of problems, in 1970 the Schools Council accepted the principle of a single examination at 16-plus; a development and feasibility programme was set up. In 1975 the Schools Council published *Examinations at 16-plus: Proposals for the Future,* which raised some of the technical difficulties involved in a common examination but indicated ways of solving them. Shirley Williams, the Labour Party Education Secretary, or perhaps her civil servants, had doubts about an examination covering 60 per cent of the ability range. She set up yet another Committee chaired by Sir James Waddell. The Waddell Report (1978) confirmed that a single system was feasible: one way out of the difficulty of assessing across a wide range of ability was 'differentiated papers'. Caroline Gipps (1986) suggests that this was the first use of the term *differentiation* in this context.

A decision on a common examination might now have followed quickly, but for the change of government in 1979. The Conservatives were suspicious of a policy which might be seen as a step in the comprehensive direction. Because the Conservatives wanted to preserve the GCE O level, they were keen to emphasise the idea of differentiation. In February 1980, Mark Carlisle announced that a new *system* of examinations at 16-plus would be introduced – the stress was on 'system', and differentiated papers were mentioned, with the GCE Boards having specific responsibility for maintaining standards at grades A to C (the former O level pass grades). The plan was that the eight GCE Boards would merge with the fourteen CSE Boards to become five regional groups. Joint GCE and CSE Working Parties were set up to work out national criteria, with particular reference to grades C and F of the seven-grade system (grade C being the lowest level of pass at O level; grade F being the old CSE Grade 4 – the notional average achievement). The task of producing national criteria was not easy.

By 1982 the decision had been taken to abolish the Schools Council for Curriculum and Examinations. It was replaced by two bodies: the School Curriculum Development Committee (SCDC) to advise on the curriculum, and a Secondary Examinations Council (SEC) to oversee examinations. SEC thus took over responsibility for the arrangements for the new joint system at 16+. One major difference between the Schools Council and the two Committees which replaced it was that the Schools Council was representative whereas the appointments to the new

Committees was in the gift of the Secretary of State. Teachers' professional involvement was deliberately weakened.

In 1982 another important committee submitted its report, adding to the debate on assessment. The Cockcroft Report pointed out the very wide spread of mathematical attainment at fourteen (wider still at sixteen), and the desirability of providing suitable teaching, learning and assessment tasks for pupils at very different mathematical stages. This gave support to the government White Paper (1978) which recommended *'a variety of alternative examination papers and tests at different levels of difficulty'.*

Gipps (1986) points out the irony that teachers wanted and expected a common examination, but what was now being planned was a common system with built-in differentiation of a kind many would not like. There was a tension between avoiding the separation of pupils into ability groups (including the need for teachers to make decisions about 'which route at 14') and the requirement that the examination should stretch the most able as well as cater for the average and below average. Another tension was the conflict between having a school-based curriculum which was not dominated by assessment, and the intention that results and standards should be strictly comparable from school to school and Board to Board. Professionalism was losing out to bureaucratic uniformity.

When Sir Keith Joseph took over as Education Secretary in 1981 he confirmed the intention to go ahead with the single system, although he was suspicious of teachers – considering them to be 'statist' in orientation. In January 1984, at the North of England Conference, he delivered a major speech, much of which was later enshrined in *Better Schools* (DES, 1985). He had much to say about standards, the curriculum and assessment, and he introduced a new element into the debate about the common examination: he criticised the norm-referencing of GCE and CSE and called for:

> ... a move towards a greater degree of criterion-referencing in these examinations and away from norm-referencing. The existing system tells us a great deal about relative standards between different candidates. It tells us much less about absolute standards. We lack clear definitions of the level of knowledge and performance expected from candidates for the award of particular grades. (Joseph, 1984)

It has never been established who advised Joseph to use the term 'absolute standards', which was regarded as rather extreme. Nevertheless, the 1984 speech received some support and stimulated discussion about criterion-referencing. In June 1984, Joseph announced that the new examination would be called the General Certificate of Secondary Education (GCSE) and that courses would begin in 1986 for the first examinations in 1988. Teachers were grateful that the GCSE was – at last – established, but it was not the kind of professionally controlled examination they would have preferred (see Gipps, 1986).

The GCSE was administered by five groups of GCE and CSE Boards (four in England and one in Wales) monitored by the SEC. Syllabuses and assessment procedures followed the nationally agreed guidelines or 'National Criteria'. It was also intended that the National Criteria should be extended in the direction of criterion-referencing to achieve a system of 'criteria-related grades' (sometimes called 'grade-related criteria' or 'grade criteria'). The National Criteria facilitated the development of differentiated assessment, using alternative papers or different questions within common papers, in each subject. The same principles applied to coursework. The process of central control over assessment had begun.

The amalgamation of grades was simple: the three O level grades A–C were preserved, without disturbing the equivalence with CSE grade 1; CSE grades 2 and 3 became aligned with the old O level grades D and E (originally regarded as O level failing grades); and CSE grades 4 and 5 became new GCSE grades F and G. But some continued to argue along the lines of Nuttall (1982):

> ❝ ... that the promise of a comprehensive and liberating examination system to match a comprehensive education system has been lost, and that the system we are likely to get, after years of stultifying bureaucratic and political manoeuvring within the DES, is divisive, retrogressive, incapable of developing, obsolescent in that it is not likely to meet today's curricular needs, let alone tomorrow's, and anti-educational, in that it will not be sensitive to the needs of pupils, teachers, classrooms, schools and even society itself.

Another criticism was that the GCSE structure included subject domination of the curriculum. The opportunity for a wholesale rethinking of the needs of the 14 to 16 year olds had been missed.

When Kenneth Baker took over as Secretary of State for Education in 1986 he confirmed his support for the GCSE, despite a good deal of rearguard bickering from the right wing of the Conservative Party. Baker refused to delay the GCSE and gave some financial support to professional development. GCSE was generally considered to be a success. Some on the Right, however, still hankered after the more traditional GCE O level, while many educationists were disappointed that an opportunity had been missed.

The national curriculum

Baker's main claim to fame as Education Secretary must, however, be his creation of the Education Reform Act (1988) and the national curriculum. The national curriculum (1988) is a good example of an issue which began as a legitimate political concern, with the possibility of consensus – but the opportunity for consensus was lost when successive politicians allowed the national curriculum to be distorted for short-term political reasons. When Kenneth Baker, in 1987, announced his intention of introducing a national curriculum, there was a good deal of support for the idea in principle, although some doubts were expressed about details of implementation (Lawton and Chitty, 1988).

From 1944 to 1988 there had been no national curriculum. The 1988 Education Reform Act (ERA) involved a number of dramatic changes, including a very detailed curriculum reinforced by national assessment. At first, teachers seemed willing to cooperate, but over-hasty implementation compounded by some serious errors of judgement eventually resulted in a boycott of the 1993 testing (Key Stage 3 teachers, for example, complained that the tests were both time-consuming and trivial). In April 1993 Sir Ron Dearing, well known for his trouble-shooting skills, was called in by John Patten to chair the School Curriculum and Assessment Authority (SCAA) and to find a solution. His brief included slimming down the national curriculum and proposing a scheme of assessment which teachers would find more manageable.

Sir Ron produced his Interim Report in July 1993 and a Final Report in January 1994, setting out the principles of his slim-down; on 9 May 1994 detailed curricula produced by SCAA subject groups were published for consultation.

To gain approval, a national curriculum must be accepted as worthwhile; it must also be manageable. An assessment system should, in addition, be fair, valid and reliable. This is always a tall order, and would have taken a great deal of ingenuity on the part of SCAA to deliver such a curriculum in a relatively short time – there is, for example, always a difficult tension between manageability and reliability in assessment. The problem was made even more difficult by pressures exerted on the Secretary of State, and therefore on SCAA, from pressure groups whose ideas often conflicted with those of teachers. To understand these difficulties it is necessary to look back to Kenneth Baker's proposals.

Any national curriculum has to be a compromise between two extremes: if curriculum statements are too general they will be untestable, but if they are too specific they become trivial. This problem remains:

Dearing decided to keep the ten levels of achievement (now reduced to nine) for Attainment Targets, and the 966 Statements of Attainment were replaced by 200 more general Level Descriptions. This is an improvement in terms of manageability, but is likely to reduce reliability. This would not matter if teachers had only to provide feedback to pupils and parents, but when results are used for league tables the demand for accuracy and fairness becomes paramount.

Dearing has succeeded in slimming down the compulsory content for all subjects and has made assessment more manageable (but less reliable). The new, reduced, subject content is least controversial in art, music, geography and mathematics, but the problem of single or double science was intensified; in modern languages and technology the proposed short courses at 14–16 are likely to be problematic; PE (slightly expanded) will be difficult to implement without more resources. But history and English remain the most contentious: teachers (and others) believe that Sir Ron has not succeeded in producing a solution free from political prejudice.

Sir Ron Dearing's 86-page Interim Review (plus five supplements) was released to the world amidst much publicity. Its reception was mixed: teachers' organisations had been impressed by Sir Ron himself, particularly his sincere capacity for listening, but many felt he had been given an impossible task and, as usual, too little time.

Some of the obvious problems had been carefully addressed – teacher overload on both curriculum and assessment, giving more discretion to teachers, as well as recommending improvements in the administration. These were accepted as helpful gestures, but to what extent had the real problems of national curriculum assessment been solved? Sir Ron's brief had been carefully constructed to exclude some of the most contentious issues, including the central political question of league tables.

We cannot really understand the 1993–4 Dearing Review without analysing what had been proposed in 1987 and what happened from 1988 to 1993. Although it is artificial to separate curriculum and assessment, it will be convenient to do so for this brief analysis.

Curriculum

Most teachers by 1988 accepted, even welcomed, the idea of a national curriculum in principle, but many were very critical of the obsolete ten-subject structure which appeared in the Act – subjects might be useful for 'delivering' some aspects of the curriculum, but they were most unsatisfactory as a basic structure. Critics were told at the time that all would be well eventually, because 'cross-curricular elements' would fill in all the gaps such as social and political understanding, economic awareness, health education, etc. By 1993 this had been shown to be a completely empty promise. Whilst the National Curriculum Council had produced some interesting documents on cross-curricular themes, Education Ministers after Kenneth Baker had either ignored them or refused to countenance anything not expressed in terms of subjects (Graham and Tytler, 1993). After Duncan Graham had been unceremoniously replaced by David Pascall as Chair of NCC, it was even rumoured that NCC officers were forbidden to mention cross-curricular elements or core skills. Moreover, those schools who wanted to work on the principle that the national curriculum was not the whole curriculum, were thwarted in their attempt to introduce cross-curricular ideas because there was little or no time left over from the requirements of ten foundation subjects. The second of these problems has been addressed by Sir Ron, but not the first. Cross-curricular elements still seem to be virtually taboo – the only reference to cross-curricular themes occurs in the context of the CBI recommendation, not in the main structure of the report. The national curriculum post-Dearing is as subject-based as ever, and teachers will still find it difficult to fill in the gaps between the subjects. One of the fundamental problems of the national curriculum had simply been ignored.

The second concern expressed in 1987–8 was whether a national curriculum would be a broad-based *entitlement* curriculum or would be a narrow, back-to-the-basics core. In 1988 it seemed that Kenneth Baker had won that battle. Since then the entitlement idea has been greatly diluted, especially at Key Stage 4 with art and music becoming 'options' rather than entitlement. The Dearing Interim Report occasionally used the language of entitlement but effectively demolished a broad and balanced entitlement at Key Stage 4.

There is a danger that the national curriculum will effectively cease at age 14, with some 14–16 year olds being encouraged to take vocational courses. There may be nothing wrong with some kinds of carefully planned pre-vocational education, but we should be on our guard against some young people being fobbed off with sub-standard, narrow vocational training. Planning a curriculum 14–19 is long overdue, but it must be carefully thought out in advance, not just accepting whatever industry may chance to offer. If the idea of a 5–16 national curriculum is to be abandoned, it should be because something educationally superior is proposed.

Assessment (see also Chapter 7)

The major concern before 1988 was that an assessment system of a detailed curriculum would mean that teachers would 'teach to the test', and that the curriculum would be distorted. Some of us were reassured in January 1988 by the publication of the Task Group on Assessment and Testing (TGAT) Report, which promised the kind of assessment which would eliminate the danger of teaching to the test. We congratulated Professor Paul Black and his colleagues for providing an *educational* document rather than a political one.

The TGAT vision was a combination of continuous teacher assessment and 'standard assessment tasks' (SATs) which would not be old-fashioned, unreliable, paper-and-pencil exercises, but would be carefully constructed examples of good teaching and learning with built-in opportunities for standard assessment. Much of the discussion in the two or three years after 1988 concerned the nature of these SATs and their standardisation. It was clear that a good deal of time would be needed to develop and validate suitable assessment instruments. Unfortunately, by the time that Sir Ron Dearing was invited to undertake the review, in 1993, the concept of SATs had already been diluted to such an extent that they were very close to conventional paper-and-pencil tests: Kenneth Clarke had dismissed the earlier Key Stage 3 SATs as 'elaborate nonsense'.

There was no indication in the Dearing Review of a return to the TGAT vision of integrated assessment. *Testing* is the dominant word in the Review (*assessment* is now confined to teacher assessment). The new jargon is, significantly, 'standard tests' or 'standard national tests'. Teacher assessment has at least been reinstated as of equal status to the standard tests, rather than subordinate to them, but the opportunity for a superior kind of teacher assessment has been lost.

Another bold suggestion in the TGAT Report was that well-constructed standard assessment tasks could be used for the diagnostic/formative purposes prioritised by teachers as well as for the summative purposes needed for local and national comparative data. This had proved to be very difficult to achieve, especially when the data is used for league table purposes. This problem is partly addressed by suggesting that teacher assessment should concentrate on diagnostic/formative purposes, leaving the summative requirements to national tests, but the price paid for this was abandoning the innovative idea of SATs and retreating to a reliance on the kind of tests which TGAT dismissed as unsuitable and which experts in the United States have now decided to abandon on grounds of poor validity (Black, 1992).

The real problem all along has been the politicians' insistence on using test results for market purposes – league tables – so that parents can choose. Teachers and headteachers have cogently criticised the use of league tables as misleading and unfair. Dearing is aware of this problem and has suggested research into 'value-added' schemes of performance tables. Value-added league tables are certainly more respectable than raw-data league tables from a research point of view, but are they *educationally* any more desirable? Probably not. With any 'high stakes' assessment, the testing tail is likely to wag the curriculum dog, with a variety of unfortunate consequences (Gipps and Stobart,1993). This is a very clear example of ideology outmanoeuvring educational needs. Those critics in 1988 who said that the main purpose of the national curriculum was to provide a framework for test result data for the market, may have been right after all.

Choice or planning?

The Dearing Report represented an honest attempt to sort out a mess – an unnecessary mess, created mainly by the ideological imperative of market choice. This was always likely to distort any national curriculum, and has in addition distracted attention away from real curriculum problems. Any national curriculum has to sail carefully between Scylla and Charybdis: if you make your curriculum statements too general they will be untestable, but if you make them too specific they become trivial and atomistic. This problem has not been solved.

It is clear that the political priority is parental choice, despite the evidence that choice does not improve standards overall (Adler, 1993; Miliband, 1991) but does increase the performance gap between schools. We are left wondering whether the government really wants to provide good schools for all, with a worthwhile entitlement curriculum for all, or are they settling for a quasi-market in which 'what winners win, losers lose' (Hirsch, 1977). The challenge for any review of the national curriculum would be to secure freedom from the dishonesty of pseudo-choice and a return to democratic planning.

The trouble with this kind of hasty review is that there is a need to seek the 'quick fix' – to prop up a thoroughly unsatisfactory structure rather than to start rebuilding the foundations. In supporting some amelioration of overload, etc., teachers may be tempted to accept practices which would have been condemned had they been honestly put forward in 1988.

Vocational options

The post-Dearing curriculum presents two problems for secondary schools: first, at Key Stage 3 (11–14), where the entitlement curriculum has survived but needs supplementing to a considerable extent; second, at Key Stage 4, where the school has a responsibility to ensure that any vocational courses are genuinely educational and not a second-best option. In addition, the school has the task of ensuring that all pupils have some aesthetic opportunities; and finally, that the national curriculum is transformed into a whole curriculum. SCAA (1995) has made some suggestions here which will be discussed in Chapter 8.

For too long the secondary school has been dominated by academic curricula. On several occasions, including 1944 and 1988, instead of designing a secondary curriculum *for all*, the traditional over-academic curriculum was accepted as the only possible model (or perhaps the only known model) 11–16. The result has been to neglect many other kinds of aptitudes and abilities that young people possess and should be encouraged to develop.

This is not simply to accept the desirability of retaining an academic curriculum for some, whilst developing a vocational curriculum for the so-called less academic. Such a solution is not fair to either group. Part of the curriculum planning for comprehensive schools should have been designing a curriculum which would have met the needs of all young people. The 1988 national curriculum was an opportunity for rethinking, but it was missed. It failed for a number of reasons which have been discussed earlier in this book: it was over-academic, subject-based and neglected such important needs as citizenship, moral education and economic understanding; it was also an overloaded, over-prescriptive detailed curriculum which had little respect for the professionalism of teachers. The Dearing Review (1993–4) tackled the second of those defects (i.e. the overloading) but not the first, except for an exhortation to think seriously about vocational options. The task of planning the whole curriculum was left to the schools themselves.

One view of that task is that schools should make the most of the opportunity of providing vocational options at Key Stage 4. This is not a total solution, for at least two reasons: first, the secondary curriculum should be planned as a whole 11–16 or, better still, 11–18 curriculum; second, we should not assume that the present GCSE curriculum is the best that could be offered to so-called academic children. A final point is that any Key Stage 4 vocational options that may be offered should be scrutinised carefully to make sure that they are genuinely educational, not narrow, over-specific training programmes for single occupations which may become deadends. Any courses offered by a school should open up opportunities for adult life in general – the learning society.

Summary

Secondary education and the secondary curriculum are among the most contentious problems within the whole education system. The 1944 Act legislated for secondary education for all without specifying either organisation or curriculum. Comprehensive schools developed without any kind of curriculum framework – apart from public examinations. The 1988 national curriculum did not provide a satisfactory curriculum design and the Dearing reforms have left many fundamental problems unsolved, although there are now some interesting possibilities for schools, such as vocational options at Key Stage 4. The major task of curriculum planning will be in the hands of the schools themselves.

7

Assessment matters

Assessment is an important aspect of school-based curriculum planning for two reasons: first, it is a vital link between curriculum and teaching (providing feedback for pupils, teachers and others); second, because it could place significantly more power and responsibility in the hands of the teachers. Various means may be developed to introduce *external* tests and testers, but the key figure in assessment is usually the classroom teacher.

What do professional teachers need to know about assessment?

Assessment is, or should be, closely associated with curriculum. Nearly all writers on curriculum and assessment stress the importance of seeing assessment as an aspect of curriculum design, rather than a process which operates independently. Assessment should be 'curriculum-driven'; but, as we saw in Chapter 1, one complaint about some kinds of curriculum is that they are *assessment*-driven. One example of an assessment-driven curriculum, or more specifically an *examination-dominated* curriculum, was the secondary curriculum in England and Wales prior to 1988. Because there was officially no national curriculum, teachers tended to use the public examination syllabuses for General Certificate of Education (GCE), and later the General Certificate of Secondary Education (GCSE) as their curriculum guidelines – what should have been a means of assessment became the curriculum. Similarly, until 11+ testing began to fade away in the 1960s, the selection examinations for secondary schools tended to dominate *what* was taught in primary schools, as well as *how* it was taught.

Whilst acknowledging that assessment should be seen as an aspect of curriculum planning, a number of writers have pointed out that assessment in schools has a number of different, sometimes conflicting, functions. Gipps and Stobart (1993) have, for example, put forward a six-fold classification of the *uses* of assessment:

- **screening** (testing to detect special needs);
- **diagnosis** (identifying strengths and weaknesses);
- **record-keeping** (often based on standardised tests);
- **feedback** on performance (to teachers, headteachers, LEAs);
- **certification** (providing a qualification);
- **selection** (for entry to secondary school, further education or higher education).

Uses and forms of assessment

Screening. Screening is the process of testing children, usually in groups or classes, in order to identify those who might have special learning needs. Typically a primary school might have a programme for testing all seven-year-old pupils in order to decide, for example, whether any had problems of hearing or eyesight which could impede their educational progress. But such tests are fairly crude instruments, and a good school would certainly consult the class teacher (and perhaps others) before taking any further action. No test is infallible.

Diagnosis. A diagnostic test is designed to check on individual children's strengths and weaknesses. A pupil might, for example, be having difficulties in reading or arithmetic. A diagnostic test would identify specific problems and help the teacher to take remedial action.

Record-keeping. Gipps *et al* (1983) found this to be the most common form of testing in English primary schools at that time. The tests tended to be *standardised* tests of reading, mathematics and verbal reasoning bought from specialist publishers. This research was carried out before the national curriculum was introduced following the Education Reform Act (1988), and it may well be that such use of standardised tests has been displaced by the standard testing (STs) which is now a requirement in maintained schools. But Gipps and Stobart (1993) pointed out that the attitudes of teachers towards testing in both the USA and Ireland were similar to those of teachers in England: teachers preferred to rely on their own professional judgment for allocating pupils to groups or sets – if they used tests they kept the results as a record for others, not for themselves. Nevertheless, standardised tests are used extensively in many countries as a means of comparing the achievement of one child with another, one class with another, or one school with another. They may also be used within a school to pass information from one teacher to another about individual pupils, or to check on the progress over time of individual pupils. Standardised tests are, by definition, norm-referenced (see below), and the advantages and disadvantages of that form of testing has to be recognised by teachers and others. Such tests may become bureaucratic devices, but they may have some important professional functions.

Feedback. Tests used for feedback are probably the most 'professional' – at least in their intentions. Results from feedback testing can inform the teacher about the quality of teaching as well as the quality of learning by the whole class and individual pupils. Feedback is also important for the pupils themselves, for motivation and for specific information, and for the parents of those pupils in some cases. Because feedback is essentially a professional function, it does not mean that results cannot be collected and used for bureaucratic purposes such as comparing classes and schools.

Certification. Tests used to provide students with a certificate are usually associated with some kind of public qualification – that is, another bureaucratic function which may or may not have some educational benefits. A certificate of qualification is an indication that a certain standard or benchmark has been reached. It is important for employers and others to know whether a qualification is norm-referenced or criterion-referenced (see below).

Selection. Many teachers are uneasy about assessment used to select pupils. Tests may be used to select children for a type of school (for example, an academic grammar school at about age 11) or to select secondary students for different kinds of further or higher education (or perhaps none at all). Teachers may be uneasy because they think that the selection process is not completely fair, or because they feel that this kind of testing involves a pass/fail mentality that is essentially anti-educational and results in labelling children as successes and failures. Selection testing is nevertheless extremely common in most education systems.

Professional and managerial assessment

Gipps and Stobart (1993) have also made a distinction between *professional* and *managerial* functions of assessment. Professional use of assessment helps teachers educate children and complements curriculum planning; managerial or 'bureaucratic' assessment (especially testing) is used to manage the education system efficiently, perhaps producing the kind of test results that can be employed to compare the performance of teachers, schools or whole districts for purposes of accountability, or to allocate resources (e.g. for special educational needs provision, test results may be a better indicator of need than free school meals).

The decision about what *kind* of assessment to use for any specific purpose is essentially a professional judgment, but teachers and other educationists have to recognise that non-professionals, for example parents and politicians, may have a legitimate interest in testing and assessment. There may sometimes be pressures on teachers to use assessment in ways which conflict with their professional judgment.

It has sometimes been suggested that teachers are good at assessing the achievements of their own pupils but less skilled at relating those results to national standards. But governments sometimes have a legitimate need for national statistics and embark upon projects which involve complex systems of data collection and analysis. One example was the Assessment of Performance Unit (APU), the significance of which has often been underestimated. A brief summary may be helpful at this point.

Monitoring standards

When the APU first appeared on the scene in 1974, I was somewhat critical (Lawton, 1980), partly because the APU was initiated without taking sufficient account of the *technical* problems involved (see below), and partly because it did not take sufficient account of *professional* concerns. Nevertheless, I am happy to admit that on the whole the outcomes of the APU experiment were beneficial – and I now wish that it still existed. The idea behind the APU was that standards could be monitored, without a national curriculum, and without having the backwash effects of conventional testing programmes. In theory, schools would have been free to teach whatever curriculum they wished, and monitoring would have been by means of 'lines of development', not of curriculum subject matter. The planned lines of development were:

- mathematical,
- language,
- scientific,
- physical,
- aesthetic, and
- personal/social.

For each 'line', it was intended to set up a working party to specify the key ideas, concepts and skills which would be tested nationally by a process of 'light sampling' (that is, not whole classes or whole schools, but a small national sample). The intention was, at that stage, to monitor national standards, not to identify poor schools or weak teachers. Some teacher organisations were nevertheless suspicious, but they agreed to cooperate. It was seen as much less a threat to professional autonomy than the imposition of a national curriculum, and in retrospect, perhaps the teacher unions were unnecessarily hostile to a proposal which did not in effect threaten professionalism.

The idea of an assessment programme independent of a common curriculum was, of course, not without difficulties. Although the intention of the APU was to have assessment unattached to a curriculum, it was still necessary to operate with a curriculum model of some kind or at least a model of cognitive development. Perhaps one APU fallacy was to assume that the two were identical! Richard Pring (1981), for example, argued that the model oversimplified the processes of human learning and ran the risk of neglecting important aspects of experience and knowledge. Lines of development, Pring suggested, were inadequate because, although the APU did not define 'development', it contrasted learning and development in an unrealistic way. This was an important distinction, but in the end this did not matter very much: the APU never became a substitute for a curriculum and was eventually replaced by the national curriculum (1988) which was equally inadequate as a curriculum model.

The APU also ran into the problem of monitoring standards *over time*. One of the issues which arose from the specific context of the APU was the problem of *comparability:* how can standards now be compared with the situation several years before? The problem exists even in the supposedly 'content-free' field of intelligence testing. If a test were devised, standardised and first used on a group of children in 1950, and again with a comparable group in 1990, the average scores would not necessarily be the same. The average standardised score in 1950 would have been, by definition, 100; if the average in 1990 dropped to 95, it would be wrong to assume that intelligence was declining. A more likely explanation would be that some test items devised in 1950 were now out of date and therefore more difficult. For this reason, intelligence tests are regularly brought up to date. But there is no guarantee that the new items are of *exactly* the same level of difficulty as the 1950 items. The only method for updating tests ensures that they *cannot* be used reliably over long periods of time: this method is to restandardise against a contemporary population, the assumption being that the contemporary population is of the same intelligence of the old. It is, therefore, impossible to know whether or not intelligence is declining.

The same problem exists in comparing standards of reading, arithmetic and other subjects over a period of time. It is impossible to *know* whether standards are rising or falling, but we may be able to reach a tentative conclusion based on the available evidence.

The Rasch model

Item banking and the Rasch model were attempts made to overcome the problem, and it was hoped to use both in the context of APU tests. The Rasch model, named after the Danish mathematician, George Rasch (1960), is one of several statistical models used to describe performance on tests composed of a number of different items. These items are assumed to have one right answer and one or more wrong answers, so that a candidate attempting the test must pass or fail each item. The characteristic feature of the model is that it assumes that only two quantities are needed to determine the probability of a subject passing an item: his or her 'ability', assumed to be the same regardless of which item in the test is being attempted (a dubious assumption in itself), and the 'difficulty' of the item, assumed to be the same regardless of who is attempting it (another dubious assumption).

Given these two quantities, the ratio of the probability of a correct response to the probability of an incorrect response is assumed to be directly proportional to the individual's ability multiplied by the item's difficulty. If the assumptions hold, for all individuals a set of items will all be ranked in the same order of difficulty irrespective of other individual characteristics. Initially, of course, individual ability and item difficulty are not given: they have to be estimated. Similarly, it might not be expected that all test items would fall into a single scale; rather a number of scales would be needed, certainly across broad subject areas (maths, English, etc.) and probably within those areas. The construction of a set of scales based on large numbers of items (an *item bank*) involves both the sorting of items into scales, and the estimation, by appropriate computational techniques, of the difficulties of the items and the abilities of the individuals, using an initial baseline sample. The accuracy of the estimation of item difficulty depends on the number of individuals answering each item; and the accuracy of the estimation of the ability of each individual likewise depends on the number of items which contribute to his score. The item difficulties obtained are then used as the basis for the future allocation of scores to individuals who take tests composed of items selected from the bank.

Does this complicated model take us any further from the problem of testing over time described above in the context of an intelligence test used in 1950 and again in 1990? Professor Harvey Goldstein (1981) found the Rasch model sadly wanting. Part of his argument was statistical, but part of it was more fundamental. Goldstein suggested that there are basic weaknesses in the thinking behind the Rasch model. He argued that an item bank based on Rasch was inherently unworkable. It was eventually abandoned by the APU, but without finding a complete solution to the problem of comparability over time – a problem which remained unsolved with the construction of the 1988 national curriculum. Some politicians, however, still want that kind of comparability data, despite the professional advice that has been given.

Some of the work of the APU was later used in the development of the national curriculum, especially in the details of the mathematics and science Programmes of Study and Attainment Targets. Although the results from APU surveys were controversial in some respects, they provided a database of information for national curriculum 'norms' in some subjects.

Task Group on Assessment and Testing

Planning the assessment scheme for the curriculum was entrusted to the Task Group on Assessment and Testing (TGAT) under the Chairmanship of Professor Paul Black. They were only given six months to produce their report, which was delivered to the Secretary of State on Christmas Eve 1987. Their task was difficult enough simply in educational and assessment terms, but there were bureaucratic and political demands as well. Part of their brief was to produce data for the Education Department which would show differences between schools and types of school, as well as trends over time. Some politicians wanted the kind of data which would enable parents to choose between good schools and bad schools – league tables. Considering these difficulties, the TGAT First Report (DES, 1988) was a remarkably good document, but with some unsolved problems. The main achievements of the TGAT Report were to shift the emphasis of discussion:

- from summative testing to formative assessment, incorporating a major role for teacher assessment and sound recommendations on moderation;
- from 'absolute standards' to criterion-referencing;
- from fixed minimum standards (age-related benchmarks) to the flexibility of broadly defined Attainment Targets (ATs) with ten levels which permitted progression and differentiation (but the levels were not rigidly age-related).

Each of these three achievements was important in moving the discussion away from bureaucratic assessment towards more professional practices – but not far enough; and there were always technical and practical difficulties. The difficulties have been aggravated by changes in ~nment policies and wrong decisions by the School Examinations and Assessment Council (SEAC) which replaced the School Examinations Council (SEC) in 1988. I will discuss the three headings in turn, although they overlap each other on many points.

From summative tests to formative assessment

During the 1987 discussions about a national curriculum with assessment, there was a good deal of teacher hostility towards the idea of testing at age seven, whilst testing at eleven was seen as an attempt to revive 11+ selection. Another assessment-related problem was what to do with those children who 'failed' the tests at seven, eleven and fourteen. The TGAT Report avoided the concept of failure, and placed the emphasis on teacher assessment (TA) and *formative* assessment which might be useful in the process of diagnostic testing.

A number of problems remained. In order to avoid conventional paper-and-pencil standardised tests, which were known to be unsatisfactory in many respects, TGAT recommended Standard Assessment Tasks (SATs) which would rely on good examples of teaching and learning, into which assessment opportunities would be injected. But these SATs needed plenty of time for trials and teacher preparation. Unfortunately, the timetable was political not educational. When the early SATs were found to be time-consuming to administer, the government soon retreated to the more traditional solution of short, written tests. The conflict between professional assessment and tests for market choice (league tables) was intensified. It is worth noting in passing that the major difficulty of the early SATs (particularly for seven-year-old pupils) was in the recording of results rather than in administering the SATs. SEAC had made the unfortunate decision that primary teachers had to record the SAT results not in global terms of *attainment target* levels, but giving a result for each *statement of attainment* in mathematics, English, science and technology. This amounted to hundreds of decisions which had then to be converted by means of a complicated formula into a series of aggregated results for each attainment target. This bureaucratic exercise took many hours of teacher time, often after school, and made many teachers very willing to respond to their unions' call for a test boycott. These problems were not the fault of the Task Group.

From absolute standards to criterion-referencing

The Secretary of State, Sir Keith Joseph, used the term *absolute standards* in 1984. It was replaced in 1985 and 1987 by the term *criterion-referencing*. TGAT retained it and stimulated the debate throughout the profession.

The major advantage of criterion-referencing is that the focus of assessment is on *individual* achievement rather than comparing one pupil's results with others'. As a technical term, however, it is not without its ambiguities and problems.

Criterion-referencing was much in vogue with professional testers (not teachers) in the 1960s, but then for a time fell out of fashion, along with programmed learning and mastery teaching. Sir Keith Joseph needed a concept to express what he wanted, but 'absolute standards' was demanding too much. Criterion-referencing is better, but will certainly not solve all the problems.

Part of Joseph's concern was for the difficult question of standards over time as well as differences between subjects at any given time. Desmond Nuttall (1988) criticised the TGAT Report for regarding criterion-referencing as non-problematical. It is not easy to find absolute standards anywhere in education. The most frequently quoted example of a test based on criteria is the driving test: a list of skills or competencies, each of which a driver either passes or fails. But even in the simpler world of training, behind every criterion lurks a norm. *How well* does the candidate have to back round the corner? Do all examiners have precisely the same expectations? Are there no easy and strict examiners? Does the same examiner always apply the criteria in exactly the same way? (Before and after lunch?) Standards exist, but they are certainly not absolute.

In education, assessment is much more complex: there are fewer examples where it is possible to say 'yes' or 'no' (pass or fail) but more where it is possible to say 'more' or 'less'. Where it is possible to turn a learning experience into a set of yes/no criteria, we may find teachers doubting the validity of the exercise. For example, it is possible to have pupils learn the six-times table and pass a test with clear criteria. But does memorising and repeating *'six times eight is 48'* mean that the pupil can solve a real problem involving that multiplication process? In other words, is a test of rote-learning a valid way of assessing mathematical *understanding*? It was on this particular point that secondary school teachers of English eventually rebelled against the Key Stage 3 SATs for fourteen-year-old pupils and boycotted the tests.

In practice there are very few examples of pure criteria. For that reason there is now a distinction made between *strong* and *weak* versions of criterion-referencing. Weaker (or less extreme) versions will tend to avoid pass/fail decisions because teachers realise that partial understanding is frequently more likely than complete 'mastery'; where that is the case, a teacher's judgement is all-important. But with strong (extreme) versions of criterion-referencing, judgement is taboo –

competence, or mastery, speaks for itself. For the same reason, extreme versions of criterion-referencing will have nothing to do with the moderation of teachers' standards: pass or fail should be clear and unambiguous. But all public examinations, including GCSE and GCE A levels, employ moderation exercises of some kind. TGAT had very interesting comments to make about moderation, but these were ignored by government.

All of this is relevant to national curriculum assessment and the professional role of teachers. The national curriculum is an interesting mixture of strong and weak criterion-referencing, and we need to know the difference. Since the Dearing Reports of 1993 and 1994, the criterion-referencing has moved significantly in the weak direction, to such an extent that it may sometimes now be difficult to find anything firm enough to be described as a criterion. The detailed Statements of Attainment were abolished by Dearing, being replaced by Level Descriptions or descriptors. Teachers no longer have to tick dozens of little boxes; instead they are required to make a global judgement as to level, guided by exemplars. Manageability has triumphed over the bureaucratic desire for detail.

From fixed age-related benchmarks to attainment targets with levels

The TGAT Report avoided the pitfall of benchmarks and pass/fail testing; instead, they recommended ten levels, with an emphasis on individual progression. The TGAT assessment model is developmental (ipsative) rather than competitive (rank-ordered). Paul Black was able to make use of the experience of GCSE 'graded assessment' work, much of it carried out within the University of London. The decision to have a model with ten levels, each intended to represent approximately two years' progression, was in one sense arbitrary, but there was a real advantage in avoiding a model which specified one level for each year, which would have encouraged the tendency to exaggerate the link between age and achievement.

The essence of graded assessment at GCSE was that students were encouraged to progress individually, at their own pace, rather than in lock-step with the rest of the class. Many advantages have been pointed out with this kind of model: clear progression, good task-orientation for pupils, improved motivation and differentiation. The attempt was made to carry forward these advantages into the national curriculum assessment model. But compromise was necessary: the TGAT Report had also to provide the means of producing bureaucratic data required by the DES and, more dubiously, the data required for market choice (league tables).

The concept of level was a major feature of the TGAT Report. But assessment experts are divided on the appropriateness of levels as a model for assessing learning. The research in favour of levels has mostly come from graded assessment; despite the difficulties involved, Margaret Brown and her colleagues have claimed that it is useful to plan in this way (Brown, 1989). On the other hand, Goldstein and others are critical of the concept (Noss *et al*, 1989). The dispute is concerned with another concept – 'hierarchy' – the assumption that achievement of everything that is required, say for Level 3, implies capability of achieving everything required for the lower Levels (1 and 2). There are two interrelated questions: first, is the subject structured in that way? And, second, do children learn like that?

There is another important question: are all foundation subjects capable of being divided into the same number of levels? If so, are the levels so far produced truly comparable from one subject to another? (There were some inconsistencies, for example, between mathematics and science, but these may have been due to the haste of the Working Groups rather than intrinsic difficulties.) Certainly a good deal more work needed to be done to map out the precise nature of levels and progression in each subject. The Dearing Final Report (1994), after much discussion, decided to retain the concept of levels, but not to carry levels forward into GCSE grading (which retains the A–G grade structure, only loosely related to the AT levels).

Issues about level are closely connected with the notion of *progression*, which was also a key feature of the TGAT Report. Critics suggest that learning does not take place in a strictly cumulative way, and also that learning sequences differ from one individual to another. Margaret Brown (1989) accepted the reasons for doubt, but reminded teachers that the AT levels were not intended to be used for planning teaching/learning sequences; nevertheless, the levels are useful as a rough overall guide to progress.

It was always going to be difficult to reconcile the different kinds of demand made on the assessment model. Teachers wanted professional assessment to help them diagnose their pupils' strengths and weaknesses; the Education Department, under pressure from politicians, wanted bureaucratic data and league tables. The conventional wisdom in 1987–88 was that the same assessment model could not do both jobs. Attempts are still being made to square that particular circle, but it may still prove to be the problem which is most difficult to solve – even after the Dearing changes have been implemented.

Professor Black's TGAT model was greeted by most educationists with some enthusiasm. It was the redeeming feature of an otherwise disappointing, backward-looking national curriculum. Unfortunately, since 1988 the story of TGAT has been one of gradual dilution – largely as a result of political attacks and criticisms from reactionary extremists. In his Presidential Address to the Education Section of the British Association in August 1992, Paul Black complained about the 'demise of TGAT' (Black, 1992). A promising professional model has become more and more bureaucratic and political. Since then, a number of other erstwhile supporters of the national curriculum have complained about the damaging increase in political interference (see Chitty and Simon, 1993).

The national curriculum still officially covers the whole of the 5–16 age range, although, as we have seen, in some respects the 'entitlement' curriculum now stops at fourteen. GCSE is the dominant form of assessment at Key Stage 4: pupils have to take the GCSE examination in English, mathematics and science, but other forms of assessment may be used for technology and modern languages (including short courses). GCSE is also normally used for history, geography, art, music and RE.

One of the problems of national curriculum assessment arose out of the fact that the political and bureaucratic factors prevailed over the professional. Paul Black and his colleagues on TGAT were very careful to stress the central importance of Teacher Assessment, but this aspect of the TGAT First Report was never accepted by government, who wanted to give greater weight to the more bureaucratic Standard Assessment Tasks – on the false assumption that they were more objective and accurate. The consequence was to elevate the importance of external testing and to distort the whole process of curriculum and assessment.

High stakes assessment

The distortion might have been anticipated: it was an interesting example of 'high stakes assessment', which had been extensively researched in the USA and discussed in the research literature all over the world. Assessment became very important politically and bureaucratically after 1988, for two reasons: first, because it was thought necessary to ensure that teachers implemented the national curriculum and took it seriously, and second, because the main thrust of the ERA was choice. In order to choose, parents needed evidence on which to base their choice – i.e. data about 'high scoring' and 'low scoring' schools (in terms of national curriculum testing). Thus the assessment function of the national curriculum was not only an integral part of the

reform, it 'raised the stakes' of the assessment. Schools and teachers
would be judged by the published results. Not only were the stakes high,
but the national curriculum came very close to what the Americans refer
to as *measurement-driven instruction* (MDI). Gipps (1994) argues that any
test is likely to influence both teachers and pupils (if they know about it
in advance), because they will normally want to do well. Teachers and
pupils will tend to spend more time and energy on preparing for the
tests than in working on the curriculum. One unintended consequence
of this is that pupils learn those items that are most *testable*, rather than
those which are most important – the curriculum is trivialised.

Other forms of distortion also tend to creep in when the assessment is
bureaucratic rather than professional. It is more important for teachers
that children score highly on the tests than that they should understand
and even enjoy the curriculum. For some tests in the USA (and in
England, by the APU), care was taken to avoid trivialising assessment:
testers were asked to give priority to ensuring that the tests did not focus
on unimportant but easily tested content. Some testing experts go
further and assert that, provided that the assessment is good enough,
there is no harm in the Measurement-Driven Instruction model. If the
assessment is better than 'normal' teaching, then MDI improves
standards. Readers may see the similarity between this argument and the
discussion of 'teacher-proof' curriculum materials discussed in Chapter
2. In both cases professional teachers lose out to the central controllers.

Airasian (1988) encouraged teachers and administrators to think
about assessment in terms of two basic factors: standards as well as stakes,
each of which could be high or low. In the UK, for example, the A level
examination is high both in terms of standards and stakes (it is difficult
to pass, and much hinges on the result – a job or a university place).
Some politicians and others like it because it keeps standards high in
schools and makes pupils work harder. But the disadvantage of such an
examination is that about 30 per cent of candidates fail. It has, therefore,
often been described as a failure system which is unfair and wasteful.
Although it is necessary to use American research results with care, there
may be some general lessons to be learnt from the research. What the
mass of evidence amounts to is that there are always disadvantages in
high stakes testing. In the particular case of the national curriculum,
another disadvantage of MDI becomes evident: the fact that the control
of assessment was taken away from teachers and placed in the hands of a
centralised bureaucracy.

Caroline Gipps (1984) quotes with considerable effect the comments
made by Edmond Holmes (1911) – whose influence was referred to in
Chapter 5 – who condemned the system of Payment by Results:

❡ What the Department did to the teacher, it compelled him to do to the child. The teacher who is the slave of another's will cannot carry out his instructions except by making his pupils the slaves of his own will. The teacher who has been deprived by his superiors of freedom, initiative, and responsibility, cannot carry out his instructions except by depriving his pupils of the same vital qualities ...

Authentic assessment

In North America there is some pressure to develop an alternative model: 'authentic assessment'. This is a blanket term which tends to mean any kind of assessment closer to the reality of the classroom, which avoids the damaging side-effects of 'artificial' tests such as multiple-choice and other 'objective', standardised tests. In the UK this would mean paying more attention to teacher assessment, allowing more continuous assessment or coursework, and moving in the direction of the performance-based testing more common in assessing vocational qualifications.

One of the strange contradictions of the 1980s and 1990s was that whilst the government continued to regard A level as the 'gold standard' (despite the obvious disadvantages discussed above), there was at the same time official encouragement given to the more 'authentic' and professional alternatives in the form of the performance-based assessment of national vocational qualifications (NVQs and GNVQs).

A possible move in the opposite direction is the continued attention paid to league tables – the performance tables of results either using national curriculum assessment or GCSE and A level results. There have always been convincing professional objections to such published comparisons, on the grounds that they tell us more about the social class of the pupil intake than the quality of the teaching. Having denied this argument for many years, more recently the official reaction has been to accept that if league tables are to be used to make comparisons, they should rely on 'value-added' statistics rather than raw scores.

Value-added

The DFE (1995) produced an interesting document, *Value Added in Education*, which was described as a briefing paper, endeavouring to clarify some of the issues involved. It began with a useful but not uncontroversial definition:

❧ The term 'value-added' in education is shorthand for what schools and colleges add to their pupils' and students' knowledge, skills and understanding between one age and another. The object of trying to develop ways of measuring is to allow us to **compare the changes in attainment over time of pupils or students in a particular school or college with those of the wider student population**. (bold as in the original)

We are told that value-added measures could be used nationally (to provide a baseline for comparisons) and locally to compare results within and between schools and colleges:

❧ Measurement of pupils' or students' achievement over a period has to start from a baseline of **prior attainment.** The Government's aim is to develop straightforward measures of changes in the achievement of the same pupils or students at the end of each stage of their education by reference to their prior attainment. This is a better reflection of schools' achievements than raw performance tables since the effects of socio-economic factors will be largely cancelled out: the progress pupils make will be measured against their own previous levels of attainment, not against the results of pupils from different backgrounds.

The last sentence is, of course, an acknowledgement that the earlier criticisms of league tables were justified, although they had been resisted for several years.

The pamphlet goes on to specify three criteria for national value-added measures:

1   They must be based firmly on the differences in pupils' actual achievements measured against a 'clear and consistent' national standard;
2   they must use data which are accurate and simple to collect so as to avoid additional burdens; and
3   they must be intelligible to non-specialists.

There are a few problems here. First, we should not pretend that our measures (whether national curriculum, or GCSE/GCE) are more accurate and consistent than they really are. 'Rough and ready' might be a better description than 'clear and consistent'. A second difficulty is that:

❧ The transition from one type of measure to another, for example, from National Curriculum assessment results at KS 3 to GCSE grades two years later, will complicate the calculation of value added ... the interpretation of average differences between schools and colleges also needs to take account of the scale of variations that may occur simply by chance. This will be particularly important with small primary schools.

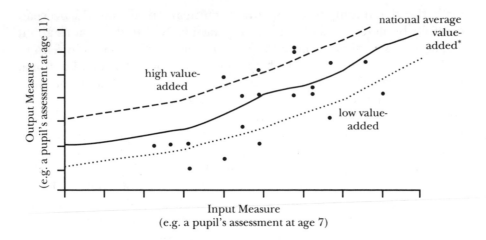

* 50% of all pupil's results will lie between the dotted lines. 25% in the 'high value-added region', and 25% in the 'low value-added' region.

Figure 1: *How to measure value-added*

❝ Because of these inherent difficulties, it is not likely to be possible to measure value-added with sufficient accuracy to put institutions in a simple rank order. It should, however, be possible to establish whether an institution's value added is above or below the national average by an amount that is statistically significant. (DFE, 1995)

Professional teachers have, however, been warned that *no* system using that kind of data should be given more credibility than it deserves – and the pamphlet itself also adds a word of caution (in the 'Technical Annex'):

❝ The concept of value-added is well established in economics. It describes the contribution to output of the production unit or industry for which it is measured. It is defined as the differences between the value of output of the production unit and the cost of raw materials and other goods and services used by the unit. Contributions by all units may be summed together to produce an aggregate (Gross Domestic Production) for the whole economy.

Attempts to apply this concept in education immediately face the problem that there is no universally acceptable measure of value. The various factors contributing towards pupil or student attainment have to be measured in different ways, using different units of measurement, many of which cannot be expressed in financial or market value terms. One cannot, therefore subtract total inputs from total outputs in a straightforward manner; more sophisticated, and perhaps less readily understood, methods have to be used.

Both the document itself and the Technical Annex should be read carefully by all teachers who are in any way involved in discussions about league tables or about value-added. There may be advantages in schools looking at their results and making comparisons with local and national figures, but the figures will need careful interpretation. Schools may find that some of the detailed results are more revealing than crude aggregations: for example, it may be helpful for a school to know that the value-added measures indicate that they are better at raising the attainment of girls rather than boys, or that the school appears to favour candidates with higher prior attainment. Value-added measures can also indicate that some departments in a secondary school achieve better value-added results than others. All such indicators need to be treated with caution, but they should not be dismissed without careful analysis.

With value-added measures we have another development which could become either an instrument for further central control and accountability, or a way of enhancing the professional skills and empowerment of the teachers.

Summary

In recent years, knowledge of assessment processes has necessarily become part of a teacher's professional expertise. Teachers need to be familiar with the different uses of assessment, and also to be aware of the tension between professional requirements and managerial needs. Some central innovations have been important, such as the APU from 1974 and the TGAT Report in 1988. The dangers of 'high stakes' testing and 'measurement-driven instruction' have been pointed out. All teachers are now affected by assessment of various kinds – including the possibility of being judged on the basis of unfair performance tables of league tables.

8

From the national curriculum to the whole curriculum

In earlier chapters I have described the 1988 national curriculum and some of its problems. The tension between bureaucratic-political demands on the curriculum and the professional concerns of teachers reached crisis point in 1993 when the teachers' professional organisations briefly acted in concert to boycott the time-consuming but invalid tests at Key Stage 1 and Key Stage 3. The political solution was to call in Sir Ron Dearing, better known for his ability to handle a difficult workforce than his educational expertise, to pour oil on the very troubled waters. Dearing received his remit from the Secretary of State, John Patten, whose attacks on teacher professionalism had made him extremely unpopular. The brief was in the form of four questions:

1   What is the scope for slimming down the curriculum?
2   What is the future of the ten-level scale?
3   How can testing arrangements be simplified?
4   How can the central administration of the national curriculum and testing arrangements be improved?

Dearing consulted widely and listened carefully. Teachers generally agreed that the national curriculum was over-prescriptive and too detailed. They also confirmed that the reporting of assessment needed to be simplified.

Sir Ron produced his Interim Report (which was still consultative) in July 1993 and a Final Report in January 1994, setting out the principles of his slim-down. The government quickly accepted the Report in full and began the process of implementation. On 9 May detailed curricula produced by SCAA subject groups were published for consultation. Dearing showed that two important lessons had been learned: *The work on revising the curricula will need to be coordinated carefully if it is to be carried through quickly and efficiently' (p. 38);* and *'The work on slimming down the statutory content of the programmes of study, must, however, include teachers and headteachers so that the new curricula can be grounded in the realities of the classroom and school planning and management'* (p.39). This was a positive step in the direction of accepting, even encouraging, teacher professionalism. But Dearing was not so strong when it came to the curriculum itself.

The background to the national curriculum problem was a complex mixture of political and professional concerns. In 1987–8, many teachers had been critical of the ten-subject structure proposed by Kenneth Baker, partly because some of the most important aspects of our culture were excluded. Critics were told by NCC that all would be well eventually because 'cross-curricular elements' would provide for important areas such as citizenship and health education. By 1994 this had been shown to be an empty promise. Those schools which declared that the national curriculum was not the whole curriculum were thwarted in their desire for breadth because the timetable was already overcrowded. The problem of time was addressed by Dearing in his Review – but not the question of giving greater importance to objectives outside the foundation subjects. The problem was almost completely ignored in both the Dearing Reports, and at a SCAA Conference in January 1994 Sir Ron Dearing and his Chief Executive, Chris Woodhead, clearly showed that cross-curricular elements did not feature in their list of priorities. A fundamental defect of the 1988 curriculum was ignored.

The second concern in 1987–8 was whether the national curriculum would be a broad-based 'entitlement' curriculum or a narrow, back-to-basics core. In 1988 it seemed that Kenneth Baker had been converted to the notion of a broad and balanced curriculum, but since then the entitlement idea has gradually been diluted, especially at Key Stage 4, with art and music becoming optional when Kenneth Clarke was Education Secretary; history and geography now also become optional (Dearing, 1994). Dearing occasionally used the language of entitlement for Key Stages 1 to 3, but abandoned the principle of entitlement to a broad and balanced curriculum at Key Stage 4.

This move from entitlement to options was decided upon partly to encourage pupils to take vocational courses at Key Stage 4. There may be nothing wrong with some kinds of carefully planned pre-vocational education, but there is a risk that young people will be offered sub-standard, narrow vocational training. I will return to this problem later.

The Dearing Review did not solve the curriculum problems but gave schools more 'free' time. He reaffirmed the doctrine that the National

Curriculum is not the whole curriculum – schools have a responsibility to transform the national curriculum into a coherent school-based plan. The implications are somewhat different for primary schools, secondary (Key Stage 3) and Key Stage 4/GCSE.

Outside the core subjects (English, mathematics and science) the mandatory curriculum at Key Stages 1–3 has been slimmed down, releasing about 20 per cent of time for schools to use in their school-based curriculum planning. For primary schools the amount of statutory assessment was reduced: for example, the assessment of science at Key Stage 1 was to be based solely on teachers' judgements of classroom work. No external assessment was required in technology, history, geography, music, art and PE. Where Key Stage 1 work was tested externally, the results of the tests would rank equally with teacher assessment and both would be reported to parents and included in school prospectuses (but there would be no performance tables for Key Stage 1 results). The testing for Key Stage 1 was limited to reading, writing, spelling, handwriting and number. This meant that the time spent on testing and marking was reduced. The reporting of statutory assessment to parents was retained for English, mathematics and science. For other subjects, schools are to decide on how results or progress should be reported to parents. At Key Stage 2, testing would initially be limited to the core subjects and would not last more than about four and a half hours. The administration of testing and recording was made simpler – no ticklists for detailed objectives and no need to keep quantities of pupils' work as evidence to back the teacher assessment.

In January 1996, the School Curriculum and Assessment Authority (SCAA) organised a national symposium on 'Education for Adult Life'. Sir Ron Dearing opened the conference by stating his concern for *'the way our civilisation is going'*. The Chief Executive of SCAA, Nick Tate, captured the headlines in the press by suggesting that moral relativism had weakened our belief and value system and that teachers were often reluctant to impose their values on the pupils. It was the task of SCAA as the official custodian of the curriculum to try to put this right by trying to establish broader national agreement on the values that society would authorise schools to teach. This would involve an action programme clarifying the issues involved and proposing a way forward. He mentioned personal and social education (PSE) as a possible area for development, not least because it was the object of much criticism by OFSTED – more PSE lessons were graded as 'less than satisfactory' than any other area of the curriculum. One of the background papers for the symposium was SCAA Discussion Paper No. 3 *Spiritual and Moral Development,* which was discussed briefly in Chapter 4. Much of the discussion at the symposium ranged wider, however – covering citizenship and other aspects of what was increasingly referred to as SMSC (Spiritual, Moral, Social, Cultural Development). It was made clear that this aspect of the curriculum – beyond the national curriculum – was going to receive much more attention in the future, especially by OFSTED.

It would be splendid to be able now to design a curriculum from first principles, but given the promise that the national curriculum will remain unchanged for five years, the short-term strategy must be to fill the gaps in the national curriculum in a way which will provide a more balanced coherent curriculum – starting with the National Curriculum Council documents but going beyond them. The problem is different in some respects for primary and secondary schools (and for Key Stages 3 and 4).

Primary school-based curriculum planning

Primary schools will have two major decisions to take (and they will normally take them in the context of the School Development Plan – see Chapter 9). The first decision concerns curriculum organisation, the second curriculum content.

(a) Organisation

In Chapter 5 it was clear that the introduction of a national curriculum was seen by some as an attempt to encourage schools to focus more on content, and less on process: the national curriculum appeared to give *subjects* priority over integration or more holistic understanding. By reducing the amount of detailed prescription, Dearing has mitigated the problem to some extent, but it still exists. At Key Stage 1 a good deal of subject *content* is still prescribed, but the national curriculum Orders carefully avoid telling primary schools how to organise teaching and learning – the *curriculum*. It will not, however, be appropriate for each teacher to make a decision about curriculum organisation in isolation: there will need to be a school policy worked out professionally and collectively and related to the School Development Plan (SDP). At Key Stage 1 it would still be possible to have a completely integrated curriculum, but by the end of Key Stage 2 it is likely that some subject-specific teaching and learning will be planned. And there is some evidence that at that stage specialist teaching is related to higher levels of achievement.

It would also appear to be the case (Millet, 1996) that primary teachers (at Key Stage 2) are uneasy about teaching all the nine foundation subjects and RE, especially up to the levels appropriate to some of the most able pupils. Schools need to discuss this problem, partly as a question of the professional development of the teaching staff, and partly from the point of view of having some semi-specialist teachers to undertake some of the teaching themselves and to act as coordinators for that area of the curriculum. Many schools have similarly found it beneficial to have Special Education Needs coordinators (SENCOs). For these purposes it will be important to have a policy on professional development for all teachers carefully related to the SDP.

(b) Content

How to fit in the extra content connected with SMSC and the other areas discussed in Chapter 4?

The school has to develop a policy about selecting non-statutory content which will be discussed by all teachers. This is, of course, a task which pre-dated the national curriculum by many years. For example, Patricia Ashton and her colleagues (1975), working on a Schools Council Project, made some interesting recommendations for teachers planning and designing a primary school curriculum. The Ashton team suggested starting by thinking of three kinds of aims – Knowledge, Skills and Qualities – broken down into six categories:

1 Intellectual development
2 Physical development
3 Aesthetic development
4 Spiritual/religious
5 Emotional/personal
6 Social/moral.

This list has the merit of being shorter than my nine cultural systems, and teachers may find it a more practical base for a school plan. But they will also have to keep one eye on the statutory requirements of the national curriculum in its reduced form. The advantage of the Ashton strategy was that it encouraged teachers to ask what kind of differences to a child's development the school should be attempting to achieve.

Teachers, having produced collectively a list of aims, may then find that they need to prioritise them and justify their priorities. At that stage I would hope that particular attention would be paid to the emotional, social and moral development of children (i.e. those aspects not made explicit in the statutory requirements but which will be capable of integration – see Chapter 4 for detailed suggestions).

That brings us back to the prior question: curriculum design – how to organise the new aims, together with the mandatory requiremen balanced, coherent whole curriculum? The national curriculum a framework, and teachers can decide collectively how to integr additional aims with the content laid down in the programmes of study. It will also be important for teachers to discuss how pupils' progress on such aims can be assessed, recorded and reported to parents. Some aspects of these design plans may need to relate to the SDP.

Having designed a curriculum in this way, it will be important for the teachers, collectively, to review the school-based curriculum annually, and to evaluate both the aims/content and the assessment procedures.

Secondary school-based curriculum planning

The problem of school-based curriculum planning is more complex for secondary schools, but perhaps easier in some ways. It is more complex because it is probable that the number of teachers involved will be greater, and the curriculum organisation will include more options. But it is often easier because the teachers are already organised into groups – subject departments, often with individual teachers responsible for inter-subject, even cross-curricular cooperation. In 1983 I suggested that a matrix approach to 'filling in the gaps' was often helpful. That was before the national curriculum; it would now be necessary to start with the ten foundation subjects (plus RE and sex education) instead of the subjects I regarded as conventional in 1983. There is very little difference!

The Compulsory Subjects:
- (*a*) English (E)
- (*b*) Mathematics (Ma)
- (*c*) Science (Sc)
- (*d*) Religious Education (RE)
- (*e*) History (H)
- (*f*) Geography (G)
- (*g*) French (F)
- (*h*) Art (A)
- (*i*) Music (Mu)
- (*j*) Physical Education (PE)
- (*k*) Technology (T)

The task is to move from the requirements of those compulsory subjects to planning a whole curriculum.

Whether they were working with the HMI Entitlement model or with some other set of 'areas' such as my nine cultural sub-systems, discussed in Chapters 3 and 4, some schools have found it useful to map out the links between subjects and systems, thus ensuring coverage of a broader and more balanced kind than is demanded by the national curriculum.

Matrix 1

Purpose: to establish correspondence between compulsory subjects and cultural systems and to indicate some links.

Systems	Compulsory subjects	New subjects or topics needed	Comment
1 Social and Political	History Geography	Politics Economics	
2 Economic		Sociology	
3 Communication	English	Communication studies	
	Modern languages Mathematics	Film and TV/ media studies	
4 Rationality	Science History Mathematics English		All subjects
5 Technology	Design & technology Science History	Computer studies Information technology Home economics	
6 Moral	RE	Comparative religions Ethics	Link with 1 and 2
7 Belief	History RE	Politics	Link with 1 and 2
8 Aesthetic	Art Music English Literature PE	Film and TV/ media studies Home economics	
9 Maturational	PE Science	Parenting	Link with 1, 6 & 7

Such a matrix does not *solve* the problem of school-based curriculum planning; it merely provides a structure which clarifies the choices and provides a basis for teacher discussion.

Matrix 2

Purpose: to match subjects and teachers with the requirements of the whole curriculum, identifying 'gaps'.

Compulsory subjects	*a* E	*b* Ma	*c* Sc	*d* RE	*e* H	*f* G	*g* F	*h* A	*i* Mu	*j* PE	*k* T

Systems (and new subjects)

1 Social
   (Politics)
   (Sociology)

2 Economic
   (Economics)

3 Communication
   (Film, TV)

4 Rationality

5 Technology
   (Computer
   Studies)

6 Morality
   (Comparative
   Ethics)

7 Belief

8 Aesthetic
   (Sculpture,
   etc.)

9 Maturational
   (Parenting)

The purpose of Matrix 2 is to enable teachers, cooperatively, to identify gaps in the whole curriculum and to plan which existing subjects will be used to fill the gaps. At this stage particular attention should be paid to the emotional, social and moral development of children – those aspects of development neglected in the national curriculum but now being highlighted for action by the schools themselves. For some schools an adjustment to the matrix will be necessary if, for example, Personal and Social Education (PSE) is treated as a subject in its own right rather than as something left for tutor groups or pastoral care. The matrix may also be useful for deciding on procedures for assessing pupils, record-keeping and reporting the results to parents.

A school-based plan for Key Stage 4/GCSE

SCAA followed up the Dearing Final Report (1994) with a document specifically concerned with pupils 14–16: *Managing the Curriculum at Key Stage 4* (SCAA, 1995). The purpose of the document was to offer some guidance on using the time made available by the Dearing Review. It begins with a reminder that:

❝ The context for the work of schools at KS 4, as at other Key Stages, is Section 1 of the Education Reform Act (1988), with its requirement for a balanced and broadly based curriculum which promotes the spiritual, moral, cultural, mental and physical development of pupils and prepares them for the opportunities, responsibilities and experiences of adult life.

Some have criticised Dearing for appearing to narrow the curriculum at Key Stage 4 in his Review, but this document attempts to show how breadth can be retained. According to SCAA, the majority of schools they consulted devoted about 60 per cent of curriculum time to a group of subjects compulsory for all pupils. Within that compulsory element, time allocations were roughly as follows:

A norm to deviate from?
- English 12.5%
- Mathematics 12.5%
- Double Science 20%
- PE 5%
- RE 5%
- Personal and Social Education 5%

SCAA offered some suggestion for combining the compulsory elements
with new Short Courses approved in art, geography, history, music, PE,
design and technology, modern foreign languages (MFL), IT and RE.
Some examining groups also offer GCSE syllabuses in humanities, or a
combination including geography and history. Even so, it is still not easy
for schools to offer everything they would wish to – in the form of a
balanced and broadly based design – and it is essential that proposals
should be discussed with all the teachers concerned.

One of the suggestions made by SCAA was the inclusion of a GNVQ
Part 1 offered as a pilot course in Business, Health and Social Care and
Manufacturing (in 1995) with additional titles to follow in the 1996 pilot –
Art and Design, IT, and Leisure and Tourism. (The courses are the joint
responsibility of SCAA and the National Council for Vocational
Qualifications, with evaluation being the responsibility of OFSTED.)

SCAA (1995) suggest that, in deciding what to offer, the following
questions might be helpful:

6 New curriculum options:

Short Courses
- What are the curriculum advantages of Short Courses at Key Stage 4?
- Which, if any, Short Courses should be introduced?
- Should they be available for all pupils?
- What opportunities would Short Courses provide for progression post-16?
- What are the relative advantages of one-year '10%' Courses and two-year '5%' Courses to pupils and to the school?

Vocational Courses
- What are the curriculum advantages of vocational courses to pupils at Key Stage 4?
- Which, if any, vocational courses should be introduced?
- Should they be options, or should each pupil's curriculum include a vocational dimension?
- What opportunities would vocational options provide for progression post-16?

General Considerations
- How would the introduction of new courses affect other parts of the curriculum?
- What are the implications for timetabling, staffing and school organisation?
- What staff development would be required?
- What are the resource implications of particular courses?
- What are the implications for the management team?

Proposals of a different kind are included in some publications from the National Commission on Education, for example *The Classroom of 2015* by David Wood, who makes a number of suggestions about the use of information technology in ways which might revolutionise our thinking about this stage of education. If all young people 14–16 are to be provided with a broad, balanced and coherent curriculum, it is clear that very careful school-based planning will be essential.

Education 16–19

We are now fortunately beyond the time when sixteen-year-olds were faced with a choice of attempting A levels or going to work – with a little training, if they were lucky. Schools have always recognised that A levels were not suited for everyone who wanted to continue after 16, but have been constrained by what alternatives were available. Many would like to see a reform of A levels into a more integrated system (see the national curriculum recommendations in *Learning to Succeed* (National Commission on Education, 1993) or Finegold *et al* (1990) *A British Baccalaureat)*. Neither has yet been seriously considered by government. Meanwhile, there is a real choice between A levels, NVQs and GNVQs ('vocational A levels') – or even a mixture of the three. GNVQs have established themselves as attractive alternatives, despite some early teething problems and some hostile criticism. The advantage of the GNVQ approach is that it has profited from the lessons learned from TVEI both in terms of style of learning and of assessment. Whereas A levels were criticised in the Higginson Report (1988) for relying too much on the memorisation of content, the intention of GNVQs is to encourage *process*. GNVQ assessment is designed to discourage too much lecturing and close direction by the teacher: students have to demonstrate that they have planned and evaluated their own work – establishing their own ways of presenting results in portfolios that they are responsible for. Teachers are freed from the pressure to cover the content, which is one of the most common complaints about A level.

The whole question of choices post-16 is clearly discussed in *Learning for the Future* by Richardson *et al* (November 1995), which is an interim report from a project examining the 'Options for modernising the English system of post-compulsory education and training'. The interim report raises a number of crucial issues for the education and training of the 16+ age group; all secondary teachers should read it.

None of these publications offers a complete solution, but they do suggest approaches which could be discussed by teachers engaged in the task of replanning the curriculum. There are no easy answers, but implementation will be more likely to succeed if the school-based curriculum has been discussed by the whole staff, and incorporated where appropriate into the School Development Plan.

Summary

The Dearing Reports succeeded in slimming down the national curriculum, settling the question of levels, simplifying and improving testing arrangements. This has not solved the problem for primary or secondary schools, who now have the task of transforming the national curriculum into a coherent whole curriculum suitable for a unique situation. Each school will need to develop its own planning; a few guidelines have been suggested.

9

Teacher professionalism, the culture of the school and school-based planning

There is no shortage of advice on how to improve schools. Many individuals or groups have tried to produce a successful formula. For example, there was a very constructive OECD document *Schools and Quality: An International Report* (1989) which identified five key areas for school planners wishing to improve the quality of learning:

1   The curriculum
2   The role of teachers
3   School organisation
4   Assessment, appraisal, monitoring
5   Resources

Most advice-givers are usually wise enough to include a few caveats: the OECD report stated *'Education is not an assembly-line process of mechanically increasing inputs and raising productivity.'* This is surely good advice. The OECD was also careful to warn against the checklist approach: that is, having a number of criteria to be ticked off one by one. The essential feature of a school is that it has to be seen as a whole.

But we should first go back a little further than the OECD Report (1989) to put the whole question of school improvement and school-based planning in context.

The 1950s was a period of great optimism in education – following the 1944 Act and the establishment of the welfare state. This optimism, and a willingness to spend money, continued into the 1960s, but by the end of that decade there were significant indications of reaction. I have already referred to the first Black Paper (Cox and Dyson, 1969) which was critical of comprehensive schools and progressive methods in primary schools. Perhaps even more important from the point of view of the education community was some American research in the 1960s which seemed to indicate that schools had very little influence on educational achievement compared with the effects of home background. Pupils from favourable backgrounds were shown to do well at school; pupils from 'disadvantaged' groups tended to do badly; there was little to indicate that schools and teachers made much difference to life-chances.

The Coleman Report (1966) was extremely influential in the USA. In the UK, from a very different research standpoint, Basil Bernstein (1970) said *'Education cannot compensate for society'*; and the Plowden Report's (1967) regression analyses appeared to indicate that school organisation had little effect on pupil performance. During the 1970s these messages tended to be oversimplified, and, particularly after publication of Jencks' *Inequality* (1973), it was suggested that schools were powerless to make significant changes in educational achievement. It was not long before some politicians came to the conclusion that spending large sums of money on schools was a waste of resources: schools were less important than home background, class, poverty and other kinds of disadvantage. But could it be that this was because most schools were badly organised and that teachers were not trying hard enough? Criticisms of schools and teachers became sharper after 1973 – the oil crisis, and the general move to reducing public expenditure.

School effectiveness

Educationists found the evidence of the Coleman and Jencks research difficult to believe. Could we really be slaving away day after day in classrooms to little or no avail? Researchers obligingly set about trying to find the magic ingredient – *something* must make a difference. Many factors were looked at – size of class, money spent, books purchased, quality of buildings, the provision of equipment, and so on. The results of dozens, if not hundreds, of projects were confusing and often contradictory.

Eventually, a major contribution to teacher professionalism was made by Purkey and Smith (1983), who reviewed and re-analysed the data on school effectiveness and came to the conclusion that there *were* significant indicators of effective schools, which were enmeshed in something they referred to as *'the culture of the school'*. They identified ten factors, but warned that in isolation each factor was an unreliable prescription for improvement:

1   A commitment to shared norms and goals;
2   Collaborative planning, shared decision-making and collegial work in a frame of experimentation and evaluation;
3   Positive leadership;
4   Staff stability;
5   A strategy for continuing staff development;
6   Working to a carefully planned and coordinated curriculum;
7   A high level of parental involvement and support;
8   The pursuit and recognition of school-wide values;
9   Maximum use of learning time;
10 The active support of the responsible education authority.

Meanwhile, in the UK some very practical work had been undertaken with equally positive results. Reynolds (1976) had shown that the outcomes of individual schools were *not* determined by the social background of the pupils. And Michael Rutter and his colleagues, in a much bigger study, *Fifteen Thousand Hours* (1979), showed that schools with very similar intakes and catchment areas had dramatically different results in terms of pupil achievement; the researchers went on to suggest the characteristics of these good or effective schools. By 1988 Peter Mortimore, one of the researchers who had worked with Rutter, directed similar research into primary schools in the London area and came up with equally striking results. Optimism was restored: schools *could* make a difference.

There were twelve *key factors* according to Mortimore (1988):

■   **Purposeful leadership** of the staff by the Head. The Head must understand the school's needs, be actively involved in its working and be good at sharing power with the staff. The Head does not exert total control over teachers, but consults them in decision-making such as spending and curriculum guidelines.
■   **Involvement of the deputy head.** A crucial role in many schools.
■   **Involvement of teachers.** Teachers should be involved in curriculum planning and developing curriculum guidelines, and in decisions about spending.
■   **Consistency among teachers.** Continuity of staffing is important and pupils perform better when the approach to teaching is consistent from one teacher to another.
■   **Structured sessions.** Children perform better when the school day is structured, and where pupils' work is organised by the teacher, who ensures that there is plenty for them to do, but allows them some freedom. Negative effects occur when children are given unlimited responsibility for a long list of tasks.

- **Intellectually challenging teaching.** Pupil progress is greater when teachers are stimulating and enthusiastic. Asking 'higher order' questions is crucial: good teachers frequently encourage pupils to use problem-solving skills.
- **A work-centred environment.** Children enjoy a high level of industry and are eager to start new tasks. The noise level is low, and movement around the class is work-related and not excessive.
- **Limited focus within sessions.** Children make most progress when teachers concentrate on one or two subject areas; there is less progress when three or more subjects are running concurrently.
- **Maximum communication between teachers and pupils.** This meant that teachers should not spend all the time talking to individual children but should take some opportunities to address the whole class.
- **Record-keeping.** Thorough monitoring of pupil progress is an important part of the teacher's and the Head's role.
- **Parental involvement.** Helping children read at home and other kinds of involvement are effective.
- **Positive climate.** The ethos or atmosphere is more pleasant in effective schools: less emphasis on punishment and criticism; more emphasis on rewarding pupils. Classroom management is firm but fair.

But once again there was a caveat: the twelve factors were part of the mysterious 'school culture'. There is now a vast literature on school improvement and school effectiveness (more than 400 books and substantial articles at a recent count). If you analyse them, you will find variations on the theme but they tend to agree that, first, there are important effectiveness factors, and second, they cannot be tackled one at a time – school culture is emphasised as the crucial element.

Nevertheless, some critics have complained about the mechanistic approach of much 'effective school' planning. It is easier to deal with factors one by one than to try to change the school as a whole, and some schools are tempted to ignore the advice that you should not tackle a tiger paw by paw; others have complained that lip-service is paid to the idea of school culture whilst failing to get to grips with it – few can define school culture, let alone change it.

School development plans (SDPs)

Is this criticism unfair? Before trying to answer that, let me deal with another related aspect of planning: school development plans. SDPs are not a legal requirement, but most LEAs expect their schools to have plans, and OFSTED inspectors also assume that there will be a development plan of some kind.

Clearly some plans are better than others. How can schools ensure that their plans are professionally worthwhile rather than mere bureaucratic exercises? The existence of Local Management of Schools (LMS) since 1988 has made *financial* planning essential, but some aspects of SDPs are even more important than resource allocation. Unfortunately there is a danger that because SDPs are now virtually compulsory, teachers may see them as yet another method of central control, rather than as an opportunity for professional development and empowerment.

Hargreaves and Hopkins (1991) entitled their book on development planning *The Empowered School:*

> The empowered school is neither the unwilling victim of externally-driven changes nor the innovator who reacts unthinkingly to every fad or whim. It is the school which responds to the challenge of change by recreating its own vision, by re-defining management to support change and by releasing the energy and confidence to put its ideas into practice.

Mortimore *et al* (1994) describe how they set out to look at the effectiveness of SDPs. They started with six expectations drawn from the literature on school improvement (i.e. schools are likely to improve if certain conditions are met):

- Most staff and the headteacher can agree on a clear mission.
- A systematic audit of current strengths and weaknesses is carried out.
- A change plan is thoroughly thought through.
- An outside agent is involved.
- The implementation of the change-plan is supported by all appropriate external authorities.
- An evaluation of progress is used formatively to support the implementation.

These conditions were generally confirmed. But the *style of management* was also found to be very important. In addition, Barbara MacGilchrist (1995) found four types of plan, which she called:

- Rhetorical
- Singular
- Cooperative
- Corporate

A **rhetorical** plan was characterised by lack of ownership either by the headteacher or the teaching staff; lack of clarity of purpose; and no leadership or management of the process. In other words, such a plan was merely going through the motions of development planning: it was not only a waste of time, but actually had a negative impact.

A **singular** plan was 'owned' by the headteacher and used as a management tool. Leadership and management of the development process was limited. It was not completely ineffective but had little impact.

A **cooperative** plan was characterised by partial ownership by the teachers who were willing to participate in the planning; it was used to improve efficiency and effectiveness. The headteacher was the leader, but management was shared to some extent. This kind of plan was likely to have positive impact throughout the school and in classrooms.

Finally, a **corporate** plan was characterised by shared ownership and involvement of all teaching staff and of some others. There was a shared sense of purpose to improve; there was shared leadership and management of the process by the teachers. This plan had significant impact on school development, teacher development and pupil learning.

All of this is in keeping with the research of Fullan (1991) and others on the implementation of change in schools. We should never underestimate the complexity of the change process. And clearly only a corporate SDP would be acceptable to professional teachers wishing to use a plan as a means of empowerment. (There are other aspects of SDPs worthy of note: see MacGilchrist *et al*, 1995.)

I would now like to return to the question left unanswered earlier in this chapter: *Are these approaches to school improvement mechanistic?*

I think some teachers have approached the desire to improve their schools in a somewhat mechanistic way. Perhaps most will, unless they can find a vision of something worthwhile to put life into their mission statements. Missions can be extremely mechanistic if they are only concerned with measurable inputs and outputs such as test and examination scores. This danger has been intensified by trends since 1979 which have pushed schools in the direction of competition and marketing. But it seems likely that naked competition, far from raising quality, will in the real world make quality more difficult to sustain or improve. There is ample evidence that the main plank of support for market competition – parental choice – is unrealistic in our system, and is tending to lower standards in some schools, widening the gap between the most and the least favoured (Adler, 1993). In addition, real damage has been done by encouraging a view of school management that is closer to the world of factories than the world of education. SDPs can help to reverse that trend by ensuring that schools are learning communities in which parents are *involved* – not simply as consumers or customers.

Culture of the school

That brings us back to the idea of school culture. Many writers on school effectiveness and school improvement agree that school culture is the key element in the success or failure of change programmes. But they are often less than clear about what they mean by school culture. For the word *culture* to be used in a meaningful way, the term *school culture* must refer to the beliefs, values and behaviour of the teachers (including the headteacher); one index of success will be the extent to which the school culture is shared by the pupils and supported by their parents.

This definition is made on the assumption that it is possible to describe the teachers' beliefs and values, and to observe and record their behaviour. To evaluate success it would be necessary to measure, however crudely, the 'closeness of fit' between what teachers say they are aiming for, and what pupils do and what they achieve.

Such a framework is used implicitly, perhaps intuitively, by inspectors visiting schools. It is more explicit in the kinds of triangulation studies of schools or classrooms in which the teachers' views or expectations are compared with the pupils' account of what they perceive; both of which are then aligned with what the researcher/observer records as her impressions of what is really going on.

A weakness of many such studies is that they often take school culture as simple and given, rather than attempting to submit the school to some kind of cultural analysis. This avoidance is understandable: the difficulty is that culture is essentially holistic, yet we need to find sub-categories of some kind if we are to do more than indulge in bland generalisations. Bearing in mind the dangers of dissection, what kind of cultural sub-categories might be useful?

Many writers have commented on the complexity of schools as organisations: the work of schools is multi-dimensional. Hargreaves and Hopkins (1991) defined school culture as *'the procedures, values and expectations that guide people's behaviour within the organisation'*. This is useful, but does not identify the features of school organisation that should be analysed. Perhaps we should return to the five key areas suggested by OECD (1989):

- Curriculum (what teachers try to give pupils access to);
- The role of the teacher (including teaching style and expectations);
- School organisation;
- Assessment, appraisal, monitoring;
- Resources.

In each of these key areas the question of management is crucial. In the book by Hargreaves and Hopkins quoted above, they make the interesting claim that management is about empowerment, but MacGilchrist *et al* (1995) criticise them for making the link between management and culture so complete. It would be possible to look at each of the five key (OECD) areas as a set of interrelated management issues, but that would be to fall into the trap of identifying culture and management. Management should be seen as an important aspect of school culture, but by no means the whole of it.

Before taking that part of the analysis any further, I would like to introduce another cultural complication. One of the shortcomings of many studies which refer to the culture of the school, is that they use such terms as *beliefs, values, attitudes, expectations,* etc., as if they all exist at the same level of commitment. I suggest it would help if we distinguish between the deepest level and proceed to the most superficial – the assumption being that the deeper commitments are even more difficult to change than the superficial, without saying that it is ever easy to change any of them.

I propose three categories, in ascending order:

Beliefs
Attitudes and values
Behaviour

If we were to try to match these three categories of culture with aspects of school management and planning, I suggest the following very rough alignment – with overlaps:

Beliefs............................ Vision (of educational ideals)
Attitudes and values ..... Mission (statement of aims, goals, purposes)
Behaviour .... Implementation/SDP (a choice of strategies
                                                       to achieve the mission).

In other words, a team of teachers should share certain fundamental beliefs – for example, belief in the value of education as something worthwhile in its own right, in the rights of individuals to have educational opportunity/access to worthwhile experiences. Many of these beliefs are implicit in democracy or Christianity or humanism, and are probably held by a majority of the population, but more so by teachers. Fortunately, most teachers share a set of fundamental beliefs – otherwise they would not choose to become teachers. (Many staffrooms possess one cynical 'non-believer'; who adopts a counter-culture, critical role; one can be accommodated or contained, but more than one becomes a threat to the stability of the culture of the school.)

A headteacher's or a school's *vision* may be no more than a coherent set of expressions of generally acceptable beliefs and hopes for the future – except that it ought to convey something more specific and distinctive about the school. It is not likely that a 'vision' will disturb fundamental cultural beliefs – if it does, there is likely to be trouble. Transforming those beliefs into a mission statement may be more difficult and sometimes more controversial. A *mission statement* should be a list of aims and goals that are achievable within a given time. This implies a different kind of commitment and also a list of priorities which may need to be argued through – not least because there may be issues about resource allocation. At this level some teachers, and parents, may have firmly held attitudes that are difficult to change.

Finally, we come to the level of *implementation*. I would see the SDP as operating at this level although having close links with the vision and the mission. But an SDP is necessarily concerned with short- and medium-term objectives rather than fundamental questions of belief. School development planning is concerned with *'how'* – with *'behaviour'* and specific outcomes.

A cultural study of a school might, for example, see Management, Curriculum and Assessment in this way:

	Management	**Curriculum**	**Assessment**
Beliefs *(Vision)*	Professionalism	Teachers are experts	Assessment is part of planning
Attitudes and values *(Mission)*	Empowerment of teachers	Teachers agree on goals/plans	Teacher Assessment procedures agreed
Behaviour *(SDP)*	Professional Development	Planning	Specific procedures for TA

Other aspects of school culture could be dissected and reformulated in the same way. Only then would we begin to be able to map out the culture of the school and make judgements about the extent to which the culture was shared by all teachers and by pupils. The advantage of an analysis of some kind is that it is necessary to be able to state – in the context of change – the depth of the beliefs, attitudes, values and behaviour patterns.

At the level of deep-seated beliefs, it is probable that a good deal of consensus exists. At the level of attitudes and values, there is likely to be controversy but it will involve commitments which are not so deep-rooted.

Fortunately, SDPs are likely to be concerned with questions of *how*, (but even at this surface level the research shows how difficult some kinds of change are, as well as how easily some headteachers have got it wrong). Nothing should be taken for granted or treated as uncontroversial.

The general principle is that when change is involved, it is important to be able first to identify the beliefs, attitudes, values and behaviour that may be involved, and, second, to judge how firmly such commitments are held. Finally, it will be necessary to remember that even the most trivial changes in practice may be strongly resisted if tackled in the wrong way – for example, by top-down imposition rather than consensus discussions.

This kind of analysis can be used by researchers for school evaluation and by teachers themselves when embarking upon mission statements or SDPs. The important principle to be observed is that culture has to be considered holistically, but in order to do so we have to begin by thinking in terms of separate levels and dimensions, concluding by returning to the school culture as a whole (and the curriculum as a whole).

Clearly, this view of school culture will tend to emphasise many aspects of life, in addition to academic goals (although they will always be important). Success and failure will not be seen only in terms of league table results. There is evidence that parents also look for much more than academic results when judging a school. It is very important that parents are encouraged to contribute to school life and planning in a variety of ways. Some schools may wish to consider seriously the advantages of home-school agreements or contracts with parents which would lay down the duties and responsibilities of parents as well as teachers. Once again it may be a mistake to assume that agreement exists on important matters of procedure – nothing should be taken for granted.

Summary

1   Schools should aim at expressing their vision in terms which are in harmony with teachers' beliefs.
2   The art of leadership is to make that vision part of the school culture – by sharing it with teachers, parents and most of all with the pupils themselves.
3   Put in that context of school culture, mission statements, schemes for school improvement, effectiveness and SDPs may be more meaningful.
4   Education is not a commodity to be bought and sold.
5   We should resist too much pressure from the market: education is essentially a cooperative concern.
6   Parents also have a vital role to play in the education of their children: too many schools neglect to make the most of parental involvement.

10

Professionalism and empowerment: past, present and future

In this final chapter, I want to compare the situation of teachers now with the condition of teaching in the past, as well as make projections about the future. In each of those three subdivisions of the chapter, I shall look at *professionalism* subdivided into **status** and **education/training;** and subdivided into control over **curriculum, pedagogy** and **assessment.**

The past

The problem with English schools is that they are the unfinished products of the nineteenth century. They still possess some of the characteristics of the thinking behind industrialisation and the building of factories – mass production, strict routines, class-based in organisation and with low expectations for the majority.

The curriculum in the nineteenth century matched those Victorian characteristics: it was narrow and backward-looking for the elite but it was made to work for the Christian gentlemen who were to lead the Empire; the curriculum for the majority was quite different – it was narrow and geared to the production of obedient workers and subjects.

Professionalism

Status: teachers were generally looked down upon as incapable or unworthy of a real profession; Lord Macaulay described teachers as *'the refuse of other callings, discarded servants or ruined tradesmen, who do not know whether the earth is a cube or a sphere, whom no gentleman would trust with the*

key of his cellar, and no tradesman would entrust with a message'. This may
have been a little exaggerated, and towards the end of the nineteenth
century – in the *Fortnightly Review* of May, 1899 – a more favourable
opinion can be found:

> The elementary school teacher is not likely to be a person of superior type.
> He is, in truth, a small middle-class person – with all the usual intellectual
> restrictions of his class. He is, in other words, unintellectual, knowing hardly
> anything well, parochial in sympathies, vulgar in the accent and style of his
> talking, with a low standard of manners. He is withal extremely respectable,
> correct morally, with a high sense of duty, as he understands it, and
> competent in the technique of his calling – what we want is educated ladies
> and gentlemen as teachers. (quoted by J. B. Thomas, 1990)

Throughout the nineteenth century, teachers' behaviour was tightly
controlled by managers, inspectors and later – in the twentieth century –
by LEA officials. Teachers were regarded as semi-skilled workers whose
performance needed close supervision.

For most of the nineteenth century, elementary school teachers had
little **education,** low educational qualifications and only apprentice-type
training under the pupil-teacher system. This was gradually transformed
into a combination of education and training in designated Teacher
Training Colleges (separated from other students). As courses became
longer, the status of teaching was raised to some extent, but never
reached the status of full professionals.

Empowerment

In the nineteenth century there was no control by teachers over
curriculum and **assessment**: payment by results was in operation from
the Revised Code 1862 until early in the twentieth century. Viscount
Lowe (1811–92), who ran the education service as Vice-President of the
Committee of Council on Education from 1859 to 1864, said that
allowing teachers to decide what to teach would be as foolish as asking
chickens what sauce they would like to be served in. The history of the
NUT was partly an account of the struggles against the attitudes behind
Payment by Results, which had been instituted by Lowe on the grounds
that it would either be efficient or cheap. **Pedagogy**, or teaching method,
was severely limited by the payment by results system, until the regime
was liberalised by the *Handbook of Suggestions* in 1905 and even more by
the progressive version of the Handbook in 1927.

The present

We are still suffering from that nineteenth-century heritage: a divided system, relying on coercion rather than the desire to learn, with an outdated curriculum which eventually divides young people into academic sheep and vocational goats. Primary and secondary schools have battled against that heritage, but have not won. Standards are still much lower than they could be. The Education and Training Targets established by government are lower than those in most advanced countries, but even so are unlikely to be met. The National Commission on Education (NCE) was set up as a result of Sir Claus Moser's presidential address to the British Association (1990) in which he complained that England was in danger of becoming one of the worst-educated nations in the Western world. He urged the Prime Minister to set up a Royal Commission on Education, but this idea was immediately rejected; fortunately, an independent review was funded by the Paul Hamlyn Foundation (see Lawton, 1994). It has been difficult to shake off nineteenth-century attitudes and institutions, including attitudes to the professionalism of teachers.

Successive governments have been slow to adjust to the needs of the modern economy, and even when politicians and others, often reluctantly, accept the need for the expansion of education, they are unwilling to accept the necessary changes in the curriculum and teaching methods (pedagogy) to match other social changes. Thus, for example, after forty years of suggested reforms, we still have A levels and curricula which encourage memorisation, when we need core skills and higher-order learning processes to cope with the demands of modern industrial and technological developments.

Professionalism

The **status** of teachers is still sub-professional, with salaries to match. It has been suggested that one reason for this is that teaching is increasingly a female occupation, but that will have to change as the demand for equality is realised. Considerable progress has been made in the second half of the twentieth century in raising the standards of teacher education, with graduate entry becoming the norm in the 1960s, after the Robbins Report (1963). But graduate status is no longer enough, and very little funding is now available for teachers to study for specialist MA or MEd degrees – even on a part-time basis. Nevertheless, teachers have shown themselves to be enthusiastic users of the Open University facilities (as well as other universities), often paying all their own fees.

Empowerment

Despite great efforts by the teaching profession, there is still no General Teaching Council which would give teaching some of the characteristics of other professions (see the chapter by Professor Alec Ross in Graves, 1990). After 1944, control of the **curriculum** slipped, perhaps accidentally, into the hands of teachers, but **assessment** was firmly controlled by others outside the profession: LEAs controlled the 11+ examination, and Examining Boards controlled GCE O and A levels. The invention of the Certificate of Secondary Education (CSE) in the 1960s gave teachers far greater control over that examination, but this was removed in 1988 when the examination was superseded by the GCSE. The national curriculum was a move in the direction of greater central control, but the Dearing Review (1993–4) began to redress the balance, to some extent. Secondary teachers in England are trusted less in the assessment of their own students than teachers in Germany or France, where they have a major role to play in the Abitur and Baccalaureat.

Local Management of Schools (LMS) began in a more modest way by being confined to 'Local Financial Management' (LFM): the shift to a broader term was significant, putting not only greater control of resources in professional hands, but recognising that the professionals (together with school governors) should have greater freedom to plan. This was a very important development – potentially – as shown in the section on school development planning in Chapter 9.

The future

Several attempts have been made to make plans for the future. The National Commission on Education indulged in extensive but essentially modest forward planning for pre-primary, primary and secondary education as well as FE and HE. It has not been accepted by government. Stuart Ranson (1994) has outlined more ambitious plans for a 'learning society':

> In periods of social transition, education becomes central to our future well-being. Only if learning is placed at the centre of our experience can individuals continue to develop their capacities, institutions be enabled to respond openly and imaginatively to periods of change, and the difference between communities become a source of reflective understanding. The challenge for policy-makers is to promote the conditions for such a 'learning society': this should enable parents to become as committed to their own continuing development as they are to that of their children; men and

women should be able to assert their right to learn as well as to support the family; learning cooperatives should be formed at work and in community centres; and preoccupations with the issues of purpose and organisation should then result in extensive public dialogue about reform.

Clearly, professional teachers would be an essential part of the learning society. Conservative politicians use the phrase occasionally but without seemingly to appreciate what would be involved. Professor A. V. Kelly (1995) has concentrated on *Education and Democracy*, but he finds the national curriculum and much else in the 1988 Education Reform Act completely contradictory to his title. His proposals would also demand a teaching profession which was highly educated and trained.

One of the most interesting and most practical documents recently written about the period beyond compulsory schooling is Richardson *et al's Learning for the Future* (1995). They recommend higher targets – 80 per cent of the population to reach Level 4 (on the NVQ scale), and an education service which looks to the future rather than backwards to a mythical golden age.

Professionalism

We need better trained, better educated and more professional teachers, even if they have to be supported by less qualified Assistants. Given that proviso, the status of teachers could rise: a teacher's job is increasingly more demanding in terms of knowledge and inter-personal skills than what is expected of many professionals, for example GPs and lawyers. But the problem of numbers still exists – there are simply too many teachers to be accorded high status or paid high salaries.

Empowerment

We have not yet begun to make use of new technology in education – not just IT, but film and TV for such subjects as history and geography. And more recent techniques involving CD-ROM are still in their infancy. Teachers have an opportunity to be in command of these developments. In addition, enlightened industrialists have begun to demand a different kind of **curriculum** – with less emphasis on memorising content and more stress on generic skills. Only professional teachers can provide such a curriculum with appropriate **pedagogy.** GNVQs already need teachers who encourage students to direct their own learning, organise their own self-assessment and build up portfolios of work. So far this is affecting only a small minority of students, but the numbers involved are expected to escalate dramatically.

Conclusions

We are at a significant stage in the history of the teaching profession. Since 1993-4 teachers have not only won an important battle, but were consulted carefully about the peace treaty – the Dearing Reports of 1993 and 1994. In this book I have attempted to outline two ways in which teachers can enhance their professionalism and move towards empowerment. First, the conversion of the national curriculum into a school-based whole curriculum; second, making sure that planning, especially SDPs, is in the ownership of the whole staff, not just the headteacher or a senior management team. These opportunities also present responsibilities which can be demanding of time and energy. To plan a curriculum is an interesting but highly skilled enterprise, demanding considerable knowledge and understanding of contemporary culture as well as curriculum design. Similarly, writing a good (corporate) SDP requires a team who are not only prepared to work together but who can develop an understanding of the hidden features of the curriculum of their own school.

Appendix

The growth of teacher professionalism in the twentieth century

1902 Education Act (Balfour). Created LEAs. Many county secondary schools and training colleges established.

1905 *Handbook of Suggestions for Teachers.* Centralised control of the curriculum by regulations supplemented by the *Handbook* suggesting approaches to teaching.

1907 *Free Places in Secondary Schools.* 25% of secondary school places to be free.

1911 *Report of Consultative Committee on Examinations in Secondary Schools.* Supported a system of public examinations at 16.

1917 Secondary School Examinations Council (SSEC) set up. An advisory body to coordinate standards and methods. School Certificate introduced.

1918 Education Act (Fisher). Proposed raising school leaving age to 15 and compulsory part-time education to 18.

1926 *Report of Consultative Committee on the Education of the Adolescent* (Hadow). Recommended the separation of primary and secondary education at 11. Two types of secondary school – grammar and modern.

1931 *Report of Consultative Committee on the Primary School* (Hadow). Proposed a progressive curriculum for the junior part of the primary school.

1933 *Report of Consultative Committee on Infant and Nursery Schools* (Hadow). Recommended separate infant schools and the provision of a national system of nursery schools.

1938 *Report of Consultative Committee on Grammar and Technical High Schools* (Spens). Recommended a tripartite system of secondary schools – grammar, technical and modern – each with appropriate curriculum.

1943 *Report of Consultative Committee on the Secondary School Examinations Council* (Norwood). Reinforced Spens' views on tripartitism; suggested replacement of School Certificate.

1944 *Report of Committee on Supply, Recruitment and Training of Teachers and Youth Leaders* (McNair). To raise the status of teachers, suggested increasing teachers' salaries and proposed three years' training.
Education Act (Butler). Provision for raising the school leaving age to 15; education organised in three stages – primary, secondary and further.

1944 Ministry of Education replaced the Board of Education.

1951 General Certificate of Education (GCE O and A levels) introduced.

1959 *Report of Central Advisory Council, 15–18* (Crowther). Recommended raising school leaving age to 16 and condemned over-specialisation in sixth forms.

1960 *Report of Committee on Secondary School Examinations* (Beloe). Recommended the Certificate of Secondary Education (CSE).

1963 *Report of Central Advisory Council, Half Our Future* (Newsom).
Report of Committee on Higher Education (Robbins). Recommended expansion of HE and graduate status for teachers

1964 Ministry of Education replaced by Department of Education and Science (DES).

1964 *DES Report of Working Party on Schools' Curricula and Examinations* (Lockwood). Led to Schools Council for the Curriculum and Examinations, which took over the work of SSEC.

1965 *DES Circular 10/65: The Organisation of Secondary Education.* Six ways in which LEAs could reorganise for comprehensive education.

1967 *Report of Central Advisory Council: Children and Their Primary Schools* (Plowden). Recommended positive discrimination and expansion of nursery education.

1970 *DES Circular 10/70: The Organisation of Secondary Education.* The Conservatives cancelled 10/65 and allowed LEAs discretion.

1972 *Report of Committee on Enquiry into Teacher Education and Training* (James). Recommended reorganisation of TET into three cycles. DipHE introduced.

1972 *DES White Paper: A Framework for Expansion.* Colleges of Education encouraged to become more diverse.

1974 Assessment of Performance Unit (APU) set up by DES for assessing and monitoring achievement.

1975 *Report of Committee of Inquiry: A Language for Life* (Bullock). Language across the curriculum.

1976 *Education Act.* LEAs required to submit comprehensive schemes; Direct grant schools to join maintained system or become independent.

1977 *Report of Committee of Enquiry: A New Partnership for Our Schools* (Taylor). Recommended widening powers and representation of governing bodies.
Green Paper: Education in Schools: A Consultative Document.

1978 *Report of Committee of Enquiry into the Education of Handicapped Children and Young People* (Warnock). Recommended integration.

1978 *Report of Steering Committee to Consider Proposals for Replacing GCE O Level and CSE by a Common System of Examining* (Waddell).

1979 Education Act. Repealed 1976 Act.

1980 Education Act. 'Parents' Charter'.

1981 Education Act. Implementation of Warnock Report.
Department of Employment White Paper: A New Training Initiative – A Programme for Action. A year's training for all 16–17-year-old school leavers.

1982 School Curriculum Development Committee (SCDC) and a Secondary Examinations Council (SEC) to replace Schools Council.
White Paper: Teaching Quality.

1983 Secondary Examinations Council and School Curriculum Development Committee formed.

1984 Education (Grants and Awards) Act. Tighter central control of allocation of monies to LEAs.

1985 *Report of Committee of Enquiry: Education for All.* (Swann). Investigated under-achievement in ethnic minority groups.
White Paper: Better Schools.

1986 Education Act. Required all maintained schools to have a governing body with increased parental representation. Corporal punishment prohibited from 1987.

1987 Teachers' Pay and Conditions Act. Secretary of State appointed interim advisory committee to impose teachers' pay and conditions.

1988 Education Reform Act. National Curriculum 5–16. SEC and SCDC replaced by School Examinations and Assessment Council (SEAC) and a National Curriculum Council (NCC).

General Certificate of Secondary Education (GCSE) introduced.

Report of the Committee of Inquiry into the Teaching of English Language (Kingman). Proposed a model for the teaching of English.

1989 *Report of Committee of Inquiry: Discipline in Schools* (Elton). Recommended measures to secure orderly atmosphere for teaching and learning.

1991 *School Teachers' Pay and Conditions Act.* Superseded 1987 legislation.

White Paper: Education and Training for the 21st Century.

1992 *White Paper: Choice and Diversity: A Framework for Schools.*

Education (Schools) Act. New arrangements for school inspection: OFSTED.

Further and Higher Education Act. Unification of funding of HE with a Higher Education Funding Council (HEFC) for England and a separate one for Wales. CNAA disbanded; polytechnics to become universities by December 1993. FE colleges to be independent of LEAs.

1993 Education Act. NCC and SEAC replaced by School Curriculum and Assessment Authority (SCAA). Unsatisfactory schools to be subject to tighter supervision.

Funding Agency for Schools (FAS) set up.

1994 *White Paper: Competitiveness – Helping Business to Win.*

Report on the National Curriculum and its Assessment (Dearing). Proposals to reduce the content of the National Curriculum and to simplify assessment arrangements.

Education Act. Established a Teacher Training Agency (TTA) for England and Wales to fund teacher training courses and to involve schools in initial training partnerships with HE institutions.

1995 *White Paper: Competitiveness – Forging Ahead.*

Department for Education merged with Employment Department to become Department for Education and Employment (DFEE).

Sir Ron Dearing's *Review of 16–19 Qualifications: Interim Report*

Glossary of acronyms

A level	Advanced level of the GCE examination
APU	Assessment of Performance Unit
AT	Attainment Target
BTEC	Business and Technology Education Council
CATE	Council for the Accreditation of Teacher Education (replaced by TTA)
CBI	Confederation of British Industries
CSE	Certificate of Secondary Education
DE	Department of Employment
DES	Department of Education and Science (superseded by DFE in 1990)
DFE	Department for Education (combined with Employment in 1995)
DFEE	Department for Education and Employment
FAS	Funding Agency for Schools
FE	Further Education
FEU	Further Education Unit
GCE	General Certificate of Education
GCSE	General Certificate of Secondary Education
GMS	Grant Maintained School
GNVQ	General National Vocational Qualification
HE	Higher Education
HMI	Her Majesty's Inspectorate
IPPR	Institute for Public Policy Research
LEA	Local Education Authority
NCC	National Curriculum Council (merged with SEAC to become SCAA, 1993)
NCVQ	National Council for Vocational Qualifications
NVQ	National Vocational Qualification
OFSTED	Office for Standards in Education
O level	Ordinary level of GCE examinations
PSE	Personal and Social Education
RE	Religious Education

SAT   Standard Assessment Task
SCAA   School Curriculum and Assessment Authority
SDP   School Development Plan
SEAC   School Examinations and Assessment Council (replaced by SCAA)
SoA   Statement of Attainment (now obsolete)

TGAT   Task Group on Assessment and Testing
TTA   Teacher Training Agency
TUC   Trades Union Congress
TVEI   Technical and Vocational Education Initiative

Bibliography

Adler, M. (1993) *An Alternative Approach to Parental Choice,* NCE Briefing 13.

Adler, M. *et al* (1989) *Parental Choice and Educational Policy,* Edinburgh University Press.

Airasian, P. (1988) 'Measurement Driven Instruction: a closer look', *Educational Measurement: Issues and Practice,* Winter, pp 6–11.

Alexander, R., Rose, J. and Woodhead, C. (1992) *Curriculum Organisation and Classroom Practice in Primary Schools* (Report of the Three Wise Men), DES.

Ashton, P. *et al* (1975) *Aims into Practice in the Primary School,* Hodder and Stoughton.

Auld, R. (1976) *William Tyndale Junior and Infant School Report,* ILEA.

Bantock, G. (1969) 'Discovery Methods', in Cox and Dyson (1969b).

Barnett, C. (1996) *The Audit of War,* Macmillan.

Bennett, N. (1976) *Teaching Styles and Pupil Progress,* Open Books.

Bennett, N. (1987) 'Changing perspectives on teaching learning processes', *Oxford Review of Education,* 13, 1.

Bernstein, B. (1970) 'Education cannot compensate for society', *New Society, 15,* 387, 344–7.

Black, P. (1992) *Education: Putting the Record Straight,* Network.

Black, P. (1993) 'The Shifting Scenery of the National Curriculum', in Chitty and Simon (1993).

Board of Education (1905, 1927) *Handbook of Suggestions for the Consideration of Teachers and Others Concerned with the Work of Public Elementary Schools,* HMSO.

Board of Education (1926) *Education of the Adolescent* (Hadow Report), HMSO.

Board of Education (1931) *The Primary School,* HMSO.

Board of Education (1938) *Report of the Consultative Committee on Secondary Education with Special Reference to Grammar Schools and Technical High Schools* (Spens Report), HMSO.

Board of Education (1943) *Curriculum and Examinations in Secondary Schools* (Norwood Report), HMSO.

Bobbitt, F. (1918) *The Curriculum,* Houghton Mifflin.

Bolton, E. (1992) 'Imaginary Gardens with Real Toads', reprinted in Chitty and Simon (1993).

Boyson, R. (ed) (1970) *Right Turn,* Churchill Press.

Boyson, R. (ed) (1972) *Education: Threatened Standards,* Churchill Press.

Brown, M. (1989) 'Graded assessment and learning hierarchies in mathematics: an alternative view', *British Education Research Journal, 15,* 2, 121–8.

Brown, M. (1993) 'Clashing Epistemologies: The Battle for Control of the National Curriculum and its Assessment', inaugural lecture, Kings College, London.

Bruner, J. S. (1960) *The Process of Education,* Harvard University Press, Cambridge, Mass.

Bruner, J. S. (1971) *The Relevance of Education*, George Allen and Unwin.
Button, L. (1981, 1982) *Group Tutoring for the Form Teacher*, Hodder and Stoughton.

Campbell, R. J. (1993) *Breadth and Balance in the Primary Curriculum*, Falmer.
Campbell, R. J. and Neill, S. (1992) *Teacher Time and Curriculum Manageability at Key Stage 1*, AMMA.
Central Advisory Council for Education (CACE) (1963) *Half Our Future* (Newsom Report), HMSO.
Central Advisory Council for Education (1967) *Children and Their Primary Schools* (Plowden Report), HMSO.
Chitty, C. (1989) *Towards a New Education System: The Victory of the New Right?*, Falmer.
Chitty, C. (ed) (1993) *The National Curriculum: Is It Working?*, Longman.
Chitty, C. and Simon, B. (eds) (1993) *Education Answers Back*, Lawrence and Wishart.
Chomsky, N. (1959) Review of B. F. Skinner 'Verbal Behaviour', *Language, 35*, 26–8.
Cockcroft, W. (1982) *Mathematics Counts* (Cockcroft Report), HMSO.
Coleman, J. (1966) *Equality of Educational Opportunity*, Office of Education/US Department of Health, Education and Welfare.
Corbett, A. (1976) *Whose Schools?*, Faber Research Services.
Cox, C. B. (1992) *The Great Betrayal*, Chapmans.
Cox, C. B. (1995) *Cox on the Battle for the English Curriculum*, Hodder and Stoughton.
Cox, C. B. and Boyson, R. (eds) (1975) *Black Paper 1975: The Fight for Education*, Dent.
Cox, C. B. and Boyson, R. (eds) (1977) *Black Paper 1977*, Maurice Temple Smith.
Cox, C. B. and Dyson, A. E. (eds) (1969a) *Fight for Education: A Black Paper*, Critical Quarterly Society.
Cox, C. B. and Dyson, A. E. (eds) (1969b) *Black Paper Two: The Crisis in Education*, Critical Quarterly Society.
Cox, C. B. and Dyson, A. E. (eds) (1970) *Black Paper Three: Goodbye Mr Short*, Critical Quarterly Society.
Cox, C. B. and Dyson, A. E. (eds) (1971) *The Black Papers on Education*, Davis-Poynter.
Cox, E. (1986) 'The Belief System', in Lawton, D. (ed) *School Curriculum Planning*. Hodder and Stoughton.

Dearden, R. (1968) *The Philosophy of Primary Education*, RKP.
Dearing, R. (1993) *Interim Report: The National Curriculum and its Assessment*, SCAA.
Dearing, R. (1994) *Final Report: The National Curriculum and its Assessment*, SCAA.
DES (1964) *Working Party on Schools' Curricula and Examinations* (Lockwood Report), HMSO.
DES (1965) Circular 10/65 *The Organisation of Secondary Education*, HMSO.
DES (1975) *A Language for Life* (Bullock Report), HMSO.
DES (1976) *Ten Good Schools*, HMSO.
DES (1977) *Curriculum 11–16*, HMSO.
DES (1978,a) *Primary Education in England. A Survey by HMI*, HMSO.
DES (1978,b) *Steering Committee on A Common System of Examining at 16+* (Waddell Report), HMSO.
DES (1979) *Aspects of Secondary Education. A Survey by HMI*, HMSO.
DES (1980a) *A Framework for the School Curriculum*, HMSO.
DES (1980b) *A View of the Curriculum*, HMSO.
DES (1981) *The School Curriculum*, HMSO.
DES (1985) *Better Schools*, HMSO.
DES (1988,a) *National Curriculum: The TGAT Report*, HMSO.

DES (1988,b) *Report of the Committee of Inquiry into the Teaching of English Language* (Kingman Report), HMSO.

DES (1988,c) *Advancing A Levels* (Higginson Report), HMSO.

DES (1989) *The National Curriculum: English* (Cox Report), HMSO.

DFE (1995) *The National Curriculum*, HMSO.

DFE (1995) *Value Added in Education*, DFE.

Donaldson, M. (1978) *Children's Minds*, Fontana.

Ellis, T. *et al* (1976) *William Tyndale: The Teachers' Story*, Writers and Readers Publishing Cooperative.

Finegold, D. *et al* (1990) *A British Baccalaureat*, IPPR.

Finegold, D. and Soskice, D. (1988) "The failure of education and training in Britain", *Oxford Review of Economic Policy, 4*, 3, 21–53.

Fullan, M. G. (1991) *The New Meaning of Educational Change*, Teachers College Press, New York.

Galton, M. (1987) 'An ORACLE chronicle: a decade of classroom research', *Teaching and Teacher Education, 3,* 4, 299-314.

Galton, M. (1989) *Teaching in the Primary School*, Fulton.

Galton, M. (1995) *Crisis in the Primary Classroom*, David Fulton.

Gardner, H. (1983) *Frames of Mind*, Fontana.

Gipps, C. *et al* (1983) *Monitoring Children: An Evaluation of the APU*, Heinemann.

Gipps, C. (ed) 1986) *The GCSE: An Uncommon Examination*, Institute of Education, London.

Gipps, C. (1992) *What We Know About Effective Primary Teaching*, Institute of Education, London.

Gipps, C. (1994) *Beyond Testing*, Falmer.

Gipps, C. and Stobart, G. (1993) *Assessment: A Teachers' Guide to the Issues* (second edition), Hodder and Stoughton.

Goldstein, H. (1981) 'Limitations of the Rasch Model', in Lacey, C and Lawton, D. (1981).

Goleman, D. (1995) *Emotional Intelligence*, Bloomsbury.

Graham, D. and Tytler, D. (1993) *A Lesson For Us All: The Making of the National Curriculum*, Routledge.

Graves, N. (ed) (1990) *Initial Teacher Education*, Institute of Education, London.

Gray, J. L. and Moshinsky, P. (1938) 'Ability and Opportunity in English Education', in Hogben, L., *Political Arithmetic*, George, Allen & Unwin.

Hampden-Turner, C. and Trompenaars, F. (1993) *The Seven Cultures of Capitalism*, Piatkus.

Hargreaves, D. H. and Hopkins, D. (1991) *The Empowered School*, Cassell.

Hargreaves, D. H. and Hopkins, D. (eds) (1994) *Development Planning for School Improvement*, Cassell.

Higginson, G. (1988) *Advancing 'A' Levels*, HMSO.

Hirsch, F. (1977) *Social Limits to Growth*, RKP.

Hirst, P. H. (1975) *Knowledge and Curriculum*, RKP

Hodkinson, S. and Thomas, L. (1991) 'Economics Education for All', in Whitehead, D. and Dyer, D. (eds) *New Developments in Economics and Business Education: A Handbook for Teachers*, Kogan Page.

Holland, G. (1996) Presidential Address to North of England Conference.

Holmes, E. (1911) *What Is And What Might Be*, Constable.

House of Commons (1976) *10th Report From the Expenditure Committee: Policy Making in the DES*, HMSO.
Hutton, W. (1995) *The State We Are In*, Cape.

Jencks, C. (1973) *Inequality*, Basic Books, New York.
Joseph, K. (1984) Speech at North of England Conference.

Kelly, A. V. (1995) *Education and Democracy*, Paul Chapman.
King, E. J. (1979) *Other Schools and Ours*, Holt, Rinehart and Winston.
Kliebard, H. M. (1970) 'The Tyler rationale', *School Review*, 78, 259
Kogan, M. (1978) *The Politics of Educational Change*, Fontana.
Kogan, M. (1987) 'The Plowden Report twenty years on', *Oxford Review of Education, 13*, 1, 13–22.

Lacey, C. and Lawton, D. (eds) (1981) *Issues in Evaluation and Accountability*, Methuen.
Lawton, D. (1968) *Social Class, Language and Education*, RKP.
Lawton, D. (1973) *Social Change. Educational Theory and Curriculum Planning*, Hodder and Stoughton.
Lawton, D. (1975) *Class, Culture and the Curriculum*, RKP.
Lawton, D. (1977) *Education and Social Justice*, Sage.
Lawton, D. (1980) *The Politics of the School Curriculum*, RKP.
Lawton, D. (1983) *Curriculum Studies and Educational Planning*, Hodder and Stoughton.
Lawton, D. (ed) (1985) *School Curriculum Planning*, Hodder and Stoughton.
Lawton, D. (ed) (1989) *Choice and Control*, Hodder and Stoughton.
Lawton, D. (1989) *Education, Culture and the National Curriculum*, Hodder and Stoughton.
Lawton, D. (1992) *Education and Politics in the 1990s: Conflict or Consensus?*, Falmer.
Lawton, D. and Chitty, C. (1988) *The National Curriculum*, Institute of Education, London.

MacGilchrist, B., Mortimore, P., Savage, J. and Beresford, C. (1995) *Planning Matters*, Paul Chapman.
Maclure, S. (1989) *Education Re-formed*, Hodder and Stoughton.
Mager, R. F. (1962) *Preparing Objectives for Programmed Instruction*, Fearon.
Miliband, D. (1991) *Markets, Politics and Education*, IPPR.
Millet, A. (1996) 'Quality Teaching – A National Priority', North of England Conference.
Morgan, G. (1993) 'Strengths and Limitations of the Culture Metaphor', in Preedy (1993).
Mortimore, P. *et al* (1988) *School Matters: The Junior Years*, Open Books.
Mortimore, P., MacGilchrist, B., Savage, J. and Beresford, C. (1994) 'School Development Planning in Primary Schools: Does it Make a Difference?', in Hargreaves and Hopkins (1994).

National Curriculum Council (1989) *Circular 6: The National Curriculum and Whole Curriculum Planning*, NCC
National Curriculum Council (1990) *Education for Citizenship*, NCC.
National Commission on Education (1993) *Learning to Succeed*, Heinemann.
Noss, R. *et al* (1989) 'Graded assessment and learning hierarchies in mathematics', *British Education Research Journal, 15*, 2, 109–20.
Nuttall, D. (1982) 'Prospects for a common system of examining at 16+', *Forum, 24*, 3.
Nuttall, D. (1989) 'National Assessment: Complacency or Misinterpretation?', in Lawton (1989).

OECD (1989) *Schools and Quality: An International Report.*

OFSTED (1994) *Framework for the Inspection of Schools,* OFSTED.

O'Hear, P. and White, J. (eds) (1993) *Assessing the National Curriculum,* Paul Chapman.

Peters, R. S. (1966) *Ethics and Education,* Allen and Unwin.

Peters, R. S. (ed) (1969) *Perspectives on Plowden,* Routledge.

Popham, W. J. (1969) 'Objectives and Instruction', in Popham, W. J. *et al* (eds) *Instructional Objectives,* Rand McNally.

Prais, S. J. and Wagner, K. (1983) *Schooling Standards in Britain and Germany,* NIESR.

Preedy, M. (1993) (ed) *Managing the Effective School,* OU Press.

Pring, R. (1981) 'Monitoring Performance: Reflections on the APU', in Lacey and Lawton, (1981).

Pring, R. (1984) *Personal and Social Education in the Curriculum,* Hodder and Stoughton.

Pring, R. (1995) *Closing the Gap,* Hodder and Stoughton.

Purkey, S. and Smith, M. (1983) 'Effective Schools: A Review', *The Elementary School Journal, 83,* 4, 427–52.

Ranson, S. (1993a) 'Markets or democracy for education', *J. Educ.Studies, 41,* 4, 333–52.

Ranson, S. (1993b) *Local Democracy for the Learning Society,* NCE Briefing 18.

Ranson, S. (1994) *Towards the Learning Society,* Cassell.

Rasch, G. (1960) *Probalilistic Models for some Intelligence and Attainment Tests,* Danmarks Paedagogiske Institut, Copenhagen.

Reynolds, D. (1976) 'The Delinquent School', in P. Woods (ed) *The Process of Schooling,* RKP.

Richardson, W., Spours, K., Woolhouse, J. and Young, M. (1995) *Learning for the Future,* Institute of Education, London, and University of Warwick.

Rogers, R. (1995) *Guaranteeing an Entitlement to the Arts in Schools,* RSA.

Rutter, M. *et al* (1979) *Fifteen Thousand Hours: Secondary Schools and Their Effects on Children,* Open Books.

Schon, D. (1983) *The Reflective Practitioner,* Temple Smith.

School Curriculum and Assessment Authority (1995) *Discussion Paper No. 3, Spiritual and Moral Development,* SCAA.

Schools Council (1975) *Examinations at 16+: Proposals for the Future,* HMSO.

Simon, B. (1981) 'Why no Pedagogy in England?', in Simon, B. and Taylor, W. (eds) *Education in the Eighties,* Batsford.

Simon, B. (1991) *Education and the Social Order 1940–1990,* Lawrence and Wishart.

Skilbeck, M. (1984) *School-Based Curriculum Development,* Harper and Row.

Skinner, B. F. (1968) *The Technology of Teaching,* Appleton-Century-Crofts

Smith, W. O. Lester (1957) *Education,* Penguin.

Sockett, H. (ed) (1980) *Accountability in the English Education System,* Hodder and Stoughton.

Stenhouse, M. (1970) 'Some limitations on the use of objectives', *Paedagogica Europaea, 6,* 73–83.

Taba, H. (1962) *Curriculum Development,* Harcourt, Brace and World.

Tanner, D. and Tanner, L. (1975) (revised edition 1980) *Curriculum Development,* Macmillan

Tawney, R. H. (1931) *Equality,* Allen and Unwin.

Thatcher, M. (1993) *The Downing Street Years,* HarperCollins.

Thomas, J. B. (1990) *British Universities and Teacher Education,* Falmer.

Tizard, B. and Hughes, M. (1984) *Young Children Learning*, Fontana.

Tizard, B *et al* (1988) *Young Children at School in the Inner City*, Lawrence Erlbaum.

Tomlinson, H. (ed) (1993) *Education and Training 14–19*, Longman.

Tyler, R. W. (1949) *Basic Principles of Curriculum and Instruction*, University of Chicago Press.

Tyler, R. W. (1973) 'The father of behavioural objectives criticises them', *Phi Delta Kappa*, 55, 57.

Vernon, P. E. (1969) *Intelligence and Cultural Environment*, Methuen.

Vygotsky, L. (1978) *Mind in Society*, Harvard UP.

Walford, G. (1992) *Selection for Secondary Schooling*, NCE Briefing 7.

Whitty, G., Rowe, G. and Aggleton, P. (1994) 'Discourse in cross-curricular contexts: limits to empowerment', *International Studies in Sociology of Education*, 4, 1, 25–42.

Whitty, G., Rowe, G. and Aggleton, P. (1994) 'Subjects and themes in the secondary school curriculum', *Research Papers in Education*, 9, 2, 159–81.

Wiener, M. (1985) *English Culture and the Decline of the Industrial Spirit*, Penguin.

Williams, M. *et al* (eds) (1992) *Continuing the Education Debate*, Cassell.

Williams, R. (1961) *The Long Revolution*, Penguin.

Willms, J. and Echols, F. (1992) 'Alert and inert clients', *Economics of Education Review*, 11, 4, 339-50.

Wood, D. (1993) *The Classroom of 2015*, NCE Briefing No. 20.

Woodhead, C. (1995) *A Question of Standards: Finding the Balance*, Politeia.

Index